Cutting Edge Lodged In The Groves

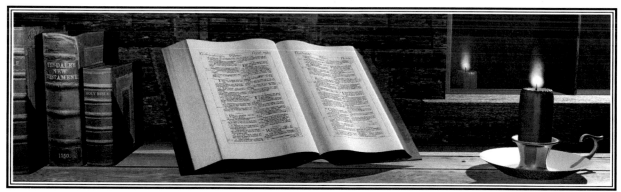

Cutting Edge Lodged In The Groves

David Bay Swings and Misses in His Attack On The King James Bible

DENNIS PALMU

Graphics and Editing by
Chris Cherrett

First published in 2006
by Palmu Publications
4719 Park Avenue,
Terrace, British Columbia
Canada V8G 1W2

Printed in the U.S.A. by
FBC Publications
3607 Oleander Blvd.
Ft. Pierce, FL 34982

Palmu, Dennis

Cutting Edge Lodged In The Groves

ISBN 978-1-60208-005-8

9 781602 080058

Contents

Conents

Preface

ndividuals and groups of various persuasions, including many "Christians" and "Christian" ministries, continue to hurl their accusations against the King James Version and those who see it as their "duty to defend" it. David Bay's attack is unique from the salvos of his predecessors in many ways, and can be summarized as follows:

1. it comes in the guise of "Defending the King James Version".

2. it utilizes a disparate group of accusers – the Rosicrucians (especially their Baconian contingent), the Roman Catholics (as represented by www.catholicapologetics.net) and the Reformed Church (especially those still holding to the Geneva Bible as the "proper" version for the English-speaking world).

3. it reformulates old questions about personalities and events regarding the translation, preparation and printing of the 1611 King James Version.

4. it disparages components such as the main title page, various headpieces and tailpieces, the genealogy pages and the woodcut letters – elements previously outside the purview (for the most part) of the KJV critics.

This rebuttal is intended to be three-fold in purpose:

1. to refute the claims of David Bay in his five www.cuttingedge.org articles, misnamed as "Defending the King James Version".
2. to encourage those believers who consider the 1611 King James Version as being more than just a good translation, and that it is, in fact, the scriptures (the inspired, preserved words of God) in English.
3. to inform those, believers and non-believers alike, who are confused or undecided about the authority and veracity of the 1611 King James Version, and who are open to new information as to why we can put our complete trust in this Holy Bible as our final authority in all matters of faith and practice.

Preface

As I drove through the northern tip of the Rockies recently, I pondered the beauty of God's creation – the lofty snow-capped peaks, the lakes and rivers glistening in the summer sun, the lush green alpine meadows filled with wildlife – and it occurred to me that viewing this canvas was like viewing the 1611 King James Version, whether it be for the first time or otherwise.

Like the various signposts along the way which are not intrinsic to appreciating the beauty of the canvas, the title pages, ornamental devices and genealogy pages do serve to provide useful information and confirmation with regard to the truth and beauty of the text. Keeping in mind one can take an analogy too far, one could also compare the twenty-one misplaced woodcut letters (see part ten of this rebuttal) to those who carve their initials into these signs to indicate their presence…initials that are seen as defacement by future readers.

For the reader not familiar with the formative years of the English language, it is important to realize that, in the early seventeenth century, spelling and phraseology had not stabilized to the point of a unified standard. For this reason, the citations throughout this rebuttal that are taken from books of that period, including some passages from the 1611 KJV, may cause some difficulty at first. A little perseverance, coupled with the knowledge that the alphabet consisted of only twenty-four letters, will go a long way toward full comprehension. The reduced alphabet meant that two letters had to do "double duty" – 'i' could be 'i' or 'j' and 'u' or 'v' were often used interchangeably, although 'u' usually served for 'u' and 'v'. The 'f' and 's', although similar, were two separate fonts. The 's' had no cross bar and was sometimes cast at a diagonal.

As the reader will see in part five of this rebuttal, David Bay's accusations and this rebuttal are set in the context of a legal proceeding. This analogy is being drawn due to the brash pronouncement, prematurely triggered, by David Bay's defrocked pastor, but which obviously reflected David Bay's misguided thinking about the King James Version. It will be interesting to see what the court of public opinion, the jurors if you will, conclude as to whether David Bay has proven his case beyond a reasonable doubt.

Part eight of this rebuttal deals with one of David Bay's vilest attacks on the King James Version…the matter of the so-called Pan Headpiece or Archer Device. After making some informed deductions on the source of this device, I end one of the paragraphs with the statement that "More investigation is underway!"

Preface

I am pleased to report that, on the day the final two books arrived that had any possibility of providing the necessary documentation, one of them, entitled *Surreptitious Printing in England: 1550-1640* by Dr. Denis B. Woodfield, published by the Bibliographic Society of America, New York, 1973 had the missing information…and a lot more! Not only did this reference work confirm my deductions about the Pan Headpiece, but it provided additional insight into the "Light A- Dark A" device and the goats head banner.

This is not good news for David Bay, the Rosicrucians, the Baconians and the Freemasons! This "late-breaking" information is brought to light in the appendices.

There is much more that could be revealed with text and graphics on this neglected subject matter, but perhaps it is best to hold this in abeyance until Mr. Bay decides if he wishes to proceed with another round of attacks.

Suffice it to say that, despite the wishful thinking of Bay and his "travelling companions", the authority, veracity and beauty of the 1611 King James Version remains infrangible… the only signs of human error or defacement being limited to errors and misplaced woodcut letters during the printing process.

One of the telltale signs of the apostasy of the times in this whole matter of defending the King James Version is that I can point to and highly recommend the writing of an admitted agnostic as being one of those few scholarly books of recent vintage that give the 1611 King James Version the esteemed place it so richly deserves. David Norton's book entitled *A Textual History of the King James Bible* does just that.

It is because of this seeming anomaly that I am especially grateful for the tireless efforts of Dr. Gail Riplinger in bringing her writing to the attention of those not jaded with the allure of modernism, philosophy or self-serving scholarship, and I also thank her for contributing the foreword to this book.

Foreword

by:
Dr. Gail Riplinger

Because God's enemies cannot find real fault with the King James Bible, they have now had to stoop to the ridiculous to try to discredit the Holy Bible. A recent web site is guilty of hard-drive hit and run, swerving recklessly around the truth of history. With a corrupt Amplified Bible on board, David Bay speeds past the facts, with stones cast at the inconsequential art work that was used to decorate a few pages of the original King James Bible in 1611. How is that for straining at a gnat and swallowing an amplified camel, full of hot desert air?

Dennis Palmu's book, Cutting Edge Lodged in the Groves, is the only one with the key information to arrest Mr. Bay's recklessness. In a day when thousands of researchers grope their microscopes in hope of finding cures for life-threatening diseases or search the skies for another star, few "search the scriptures" and library stacks to defend *the book* that can give *eternal* life and a home *beyond* the stars. Thank God for one such researcher, my friend, Mr. Palmu. He spares no expense, seeks no personal gain, and leaves no book unread in his relentless battle to reveal truth to those who have no time or resources for such an undertaking. He loves the word of God so much that he has purchased thousands and thousands of dollars worth of rare and expensive books to document the facts in his meticulously researched new book. What a gift he has given to the body of Christ!

A picture, symbol or emblem says little. Its *perceived* meaning is subjective and a projection of the thoughts and experiences of the viewer. Mr. Palmu proves from the Holy Bible and from rare books that the art work in the early KJV is representative of scriptural symbolism, in the main. Mr. Bay sees filth in these pictures. Hmmmm.

"Unto the pure all things are pure: but unto them that are defiled and unbelieving is nothing pure..."(Titus 1:15).

It seems clear that Mr. Bay is unfamiliar with the Holy Bible, yet all too familiar with occult literature. Observe the following simple examples:

- Bible readers know that the Holy Ghost descended "like a dove" over Jesus Christ when he was baptized (John 1:32). Bay charges the King James Bible with having occult pictures, because its title page has a dove descending!
- Had Mr. Bay read the book of Zechariah, he would know that God uses the eye as a metaphor. Bay has only seen the devil's occult counterfeit use of the eye.

- It gets stranger. Mr. Bay calls the early KJV's depiction of the Hebrew name of God "pagan." My new book, *In Awe of Thy Word*, citing the research John Gill in *A Dissertation Concerning the Antiquity of the Hebrew Language, Letters, Vowel-Points and Accents* (1769) traces the Hebrew name of God, *with vowels*, back to the original.
- Mr. Bay sees the devil in a picture of a goat. Is he unfamiliar with the sin offering of a goat in Leviticus?
- Bay accuses the King James Bible of changing verse numbers from his beloved Geneva Bible (Calvinist?!). The KJV did not change the verse numbers; the Geneva Bible did. The Bishop's Bible and other early English Holy Bibles match the KJV. I have all of these old Holy Bibles which I checked. I found him in grave error at every point.

Mr. Bay takes the fine books on symbolism by Texe Marrs and Cathy Burns, which I have thoroughly enjoyed, and turns them upside down. (I feel that I can knowledgeably comment on the topic of symbolism, since I have a Master of Fine Arts degree, a minor in Art History (among others things) and was asked to teach a course on the migration of symbols at a large State University.)

Bay is forgetting that Lucifer said, "I will be like the most high" (Isa. 14:12). The devil and his occult followers want to *copy* God and his Bible. Therefore *they use* some of the symbolism that God has depicted in his word. God had it first.

Mr. Bay has shown that he is not a student of the Bible, nor is he an expert on the use of symbolism. He would do well to avoid both topics. Thank God for Dennis Palmu and his expose' of Bay's sad diatribe. Palmu's book will lay to rest just one more of the devil's weak assaults against the Holy Bible and for this we can all be grateful.

Fellowservant,

Dr. Gail Riplinger
2 Thes. 3:1

Introduction

ow that David Bay has felt the compulsion to cease his rant against the King James Version, 1611 and 1619 editions, at least for the time being, it is an opportune time to examine the veracity of his claims. After hearing the pronouncing of the benediction on his five articles *"Defending the King James Version"*, one is left to wonder what David defines as an attack.

He also struggles with the concept of truth...claiming that his research and "startling insights" on the subject of these articles are the opening of "the door to ... truth".   This is pontificating to the extreme in light of Jesus' words in John 10:7-9 and John 14:6. As with many other words so carelessly used today, we shall presently see that truth comes in many guises.

The terms "fundamental integrity" and "revelations of the truth" and "what we revealed is absolutely correct" are also unfurled as banners of assurance that David's readers can carry as they travel together on the path to enlightenment.

Similar to the "truth" that Dorothy and her travelling companions found in the Emerald City, the revelations that David proffers leave one with an initial reaction of amazement, followed shortly thereafter by a sense of betrayal when the curtain is pulled aside. The Christian reader should be given pause early on when he or she finds that David's travelling companions, like Dorothy's, are a straw man, a tin woodsman and a man dressed like a lion.

Introduction

In David Bay's first article (news/k1001), the straw man arrives in the guise of a Pilgrim Parson. He says "with a very loud voice: 'Ah, we Pilgrims only use the Geneva Bible, as we would never use that wicked King James Bible from that wicked King!'"

Next enters the tin woodsman, who "argued that the KJV Bible was a Rosicrucian masterpiece and that it contained much occult symbolism".

Thirdly, to complete this analogy, it appears that a man dressed like a lion has already entered the arena, and directs them to www.catholicapologetics.net, roaring with decided pleasure that they were first off the mark in their attacks against the KJV 1611, thus having the pre-eminent position over David Bay, the Geneva Calvinists, the Rosicrucians and the Masons. Undaunted, David Bay presses ahead with his vitriol, aided and abetted by his new companions and allies. According to David, "(the Holy Spirit) forced me against my reasoning to tell this story now" and that Dr. Stan Monteith concurs.

How fortunate for all concerned that the tin man from the groves enlightened one and all that the straw man's hostility toward the 1611 KJV had nothing to do with his Calvinism and everything to do with the occult symbols placed therein by Francis Bacon and his Knights of the Helmet.

Leaving the land of Oz, we next find David bragging to Larry Spargimino of Southwest Radio Church that his knowledge of Masonry surpasses that of most Masons. This was no doubt underscored by the promotion his new DVD entitled *The Secret Mysteries of America's Beginnings – Volume One: The New Atlantis.* Here the Christian viewer is again ushered through the "door of historic truth", and into the arcane world of Rosicrucian and Masonic lore. The Christian viewer is introduced to some of the founders of astrology, the legend of the New Atlantis, occult ley lines, demonic astro-travel, and more.

Apparently David Bay believes that this esoteric, occult knowledge is a requirement in the believer's armor to stand against the wiles of the devil (perhaps falling under "having your loins girt about with truth"?).

Part 1 – The Fallacy of "Francis Bacon and his Knights of the Helmet"

ne of David Bay's main claims, in his five articles "defending the King James Version", is that "Francis Bacon and his (secret society called the) Knights of the Helmet… create(d) a Rosicrucian Bible which was designed to move the peoples of the world into the practice of a 'Mystic Christianity', ie., Rosicrucianism". This was supposedly accomplished by placing "occult, satanic symbols…in front of, and throughout, the text" for "nearly one year… after the KJV scholars had finished their manuscript". Not content with this accusation, David also includes King James in this plot "to produce a 'Rosicrucian Mystic Bible', which would reverberate with occult power every second because of all the satanic symbols it contained".

As has been pointed out in the introduction, David is not the first one to make these fantastic claims. Manly P. Hall, in *Rosicrucian and Masonic Origins* from *Lectures on Ancient Philosophy,* Hall Publishing (1929) said "The first edition of the King James Bible, which was edited by Francis Bacon and prepared under Masonic supervision bears more Mason's marks than the Cathedral of Strasburg". Hall undoubtedly came to this conclusion after reading William T. Smedley's *The Mystery of Francis Bacon,* published in 1910. Similar claims can be found on www.catholicapologetics.net.

Before even entertaining the validity of this claim, one has to question David's frequent use of Rosicrucian and Masonic writings as "proof texts" to substantiate his accusations, considering that the very structure of Rosicrucianism and Freemasonry is built on a foundation of myth, concealment, fantasy, deception, deviance and perversion. This fact is admitted to by the pre-eminent leaders of Rosicrucianism and Freemasonry.

Consider these statements alone from the above-noted lecture by Manley P. Hall:

1. "Freemasonry is a fraternity within a fraternity – an outer organization concealing an inner brotherhood of the elect."
2. "The modern Masonic order is not united respecting the true purpose for its own existence…it is enveloped in obscurity, and lies far outside the domain of authentic history."
3. "In his *Symbolism,* Pike (who spent a lifetime in the quest for Masonic secrets) declares that few of the original meanings of the symbols are known to the modern order, nearly all the so-called interpretations now given being superficial. Pike confessed that the original meanings of the very symbols he himself was attempting to interpret were irretrievably-lost."
4. "At last, in the sixty-sixth year of his life, having completed the work which held him in England, Bacon feigned death and passed over into Germany, there to guide the destinies of his philosophic and political fraternity for nearly twenty-five years before his actual demise."

Part ı – The Fallacy of "Francis Bacon and his Knights of the Helmet"

Sadly, after immersing himself in occult lore, David Bay has become a false prophet.

Consider the words of the Lord in Jeremiah 23:16: *"Thus saith the Lord of hosts, Harken not unto the words of the prophets that prophesy unto you: they make you vain: they speak a vision of their own heart, and not out of the mouth of the Lord."*

Is this being too harsh? What about Francis Bacon and the Knights of the Helmet? Doesn't the phrase "Francis Bacon – Knights of the Helmet" produce a few dozen website hits? Don't at least some of these sites such as www.sirbacon.org contain the truth about Francis Bacon and his secret society?

Before we answer these questions, it is important to realize that Francis Bacon is many things to many people. As we've seen from the quotation above, some believe (to suit their purposes) that Bacon lived "for nearly twenty-five years" after his recorded death in his sixty-sixth year.
This legend of longevity has been applied to countless others over the years…one might call this "posthumously fabricating the curriculum vitae".

Another fact germane to this matter, that David Bay neglects to point out, is the decades-old controversy regarding the identity of William Shakespeare. The vast majority of academia has long attributed the authorship of the famous plays bearing Shakespeare's name to the playwright of Stratford-Upon-Avon (Stratfordians). Others attribute these plays to Ben Jonson, Christopher Marlowe and Francis Bacon, amongst a host of pretenders.

Probably the most vociferous amongst the pretenders are the Baconians, behind which is a large contingent of Rosicrucian apologists such as Peter Dawkins. Dawkins is a featured expert on David Bay's DVD entitled *The Secret Mysteries of America's Beginnings – Volume One: The New Atlantis.* This Rosicrucian-Masonic-Baconian link, which David Bay obviously embraces and promotes, is there for all to see. Manley P. Hall wrote a book entitled *The Secret Destiny of America* while Francis Bacon's seminal work, for speculative Freemasonry at least, is the *New Atlantis*.

Another salient point regarding Francis Bacon has to do with his influence on, and degree of access to, King James. Despite the extravagant claims made by various Masonic and Baconian biographers, the latest scholarly critical biography entitled *Hostage to Fortune: The Troubled Life of Francis Bacon* provides new information from previously unpublished letters and documents that "reveals (Bacon) to be somewhat less worthy of our admiration".

His access to the court of King James is also shown to be very restricted (unlike many of the KJV translators) even after he finally cajoled himself into high office, through the petitioning of the King's new favourite George Villiers (against the ongoing objections of Lord Coke) starting in 1608.

4

Part 1 — The Fallacy of "Francis Bacon and his Knights of the Helmet"

A further point needs to be mentioned at this juncture, this regarding the real (documented) origin of Rosicrucianism and Freemasonry. Many Rosicrucian and Masonic philosophers and historians like to create an aura of great antiquity, tracing an unbroken line of adepts back to "the master builders of the ancient world". For the Masons, this is Hiram Abiff, who supposedly was sent by Hiram, King of Tyre, to design and supervise the erection of King Solomon's temple. While legends such as this make for good fiction, they do little to establish a *corpus* on the matter of actual history.

Regarding the generally accepted origins of **Rosicrucianism**, I refer to *Wikipedia* encyclopedia:
"What was known in the early 17th century as the 'Fraternity of the Rose Cross' seems to have been a number of isolated individuals who held certain views in common, which apparently was their only bond of union. These views were regarding hermetic knowledge, related to the higher nature of man, and also with common philosophical conceptions towards the foundation of a more perfect society. **There is no trace of a Fraternity or secret society which held meetings, or had officers or leaders.**"
(emphasis mine)

The first works declaring the existence of a secret society were published on the European continent in 1614, 1615 and 1616. These three publications were later attributed to a Lutheran theologian named Johann Valentin Andreae. The beginnings of Rosicrucianism in England are less definitive...some credit "the mysterious philosopher and alchemist" John Dee and others Elias Ashmole.

Again, referring to *Wikipedia*, "(t)he first Grand Lodge in **Freemasonry** (in England) was founded in 1717 when four existing Lodges met at the Goose & Gridiron Alehouse in London to form the governing body". The previously mentioned Elias Ashmole, however, "was made a Mason in 1646, and notes attending several Masonic meetings".

There is an earlier record of **speculative** Freemasonry in Scotland, 1583 being the date of the "Grand Lodge manuscript", although a public document in the form of a charter was not granted until some years later to "Sir William St. Clair (later Sinclair) of Roslin (Rosslyn), allowing him to purchase jurisdiction over a number of lodges in Edinburgh and environs. This may be the basis for the Templar myth surrounding Rosslyn Chapel." (emphasis mine)

Conclusion:

There is no proven record that Rosicrucianism or Freemasonry was established in England prior to the publication of the 1619 edition of the King James Version, the later of the two editions upon which David Bay claims there is "direct proof" of "these Rosicrucian – Satanic symbols".

Part 1 – The Fallacy of "Francis Bacon and his Knights of the Helmet"

With the above background information in hand, we can now proceed to **"the fallacy of Francis Bacon and his Knights of the Helmet".**

As noted above, Francis Bacon and his supposed leadership of a secret society called the Knights of the Helmet is referred to on a number of websites.

After eliminating duplication and vain/undocumented babblings (David's sources), we can with a high degree of certainty trace the origin of the term "Knights of the Helmet" to "a quarto pamphlet of 68 pages; printed in 1685…apparently from a manuscript written by some member of Gray's Inn who was an eyewitness of what he relates; and bearing the title 'Gesta Grayorum, or the History of the high and mighty Prince, Henry, Prince of Purpoole, etc., who reigned and died A.D. 1584'".

The above quotation is taken from a work by James Spedding, a 19th century biographer of Francis Bacon. Spedding recounts a performance at Gray's Inn "during the twelve days of Christmas licence" starting on the 20th of December, 1594.

Apparently the youth-in-residence at Gray's Inn, who had only intermittently produced masques or "revels" in the previous three or four years "were resolved to redeem the time by producing this year something out of the common way". "Their device was to turn Gray's Inn…into the semblance of a court and kingdom…and to entertain each other…with the playing at kings and counselors. They proceeded accordingly to elect a prince—the Prince of Purpoole." Spedding informs us that *gestus* means "artificial gesture of an actor". *Grayorum* is obviously a pseudo-Latin term for Gray's Inn.

The documentation for this can be found at http://fly.hiwaay.net/~paul/bacon/devices/gestaintro.html, but to make a long story short, Spedding tells us that "it is most probable that one of these 'graver concepts' in attendance on Friday, the 3rd of January 1595 was Bacon himself". Spedding also notes that "Bacon certainly had a hand, though not, I think, in the execution" of this "playful satire". He then goes on to qualify this statement by saying "that Bacon had a hand in the general design is merely a conjecture".

Be that as it may, the following excerpts from Spedding's account clearly show the foolishness in relying on Rosicrucian and Masonic adepts for "startling insights" and opening "the door to truth".

"The show being ended, the Prince in token of satisfaction invested the Ambassador and twenty-four of his retinue, with the Collar of the Knighthood of the Helmet; upon which the King-at-Arms, --having first declared how the Prince had instituted this Order in memory of the arms he bore…in regard that as the helmet defendeth the chiefest part of the body, the head, so did he then defend the head of the state, -- proceeded to read the articles of the Order; which they were all to vow to keep, each kissing the helmet as he took his vow."

After this mock ceremony, Spedding informs us that "the ceremony of investiture was followed by a 'variety of consort-music' and a running banquet served by the **Knights of the Helmet** who were not strangers: and so this part of the entertainment ended". (emphasis mine)

Conclusion:

There is no evidence to support David Bay's claim, and those of his Masonic sources, that Francis Bacon and his secret society called the Knights of the Helmet "spent nearly one year fashioning these symbolic pages in front of, and throughout, the text" and "did, indeed, direct the placement of these Rosicrucian – Satanic symbols and pages".

"For the time will come when they will not endure sound doctrine; but after their own lusts shall they heap to themselves teachers, having itching ears;
And they shall turn away their ears from the truth, and shall be turned unto fables".
2 Timothy 4:4 (1611 King James Version).

Part 2 – Masonic Deception Regarding Francis Bacon and his Knights of the Helmet

As has been pointed out in the Introduction and Part 1 of this rebuttal, David Bay for his own reasons has chosen to embrace and employ Masonic and occult lore in his attack on the King James Version (1611 and 1619 editions). What this does, in effect, is give the appearance of historical legitimacy to a plethora of arcane writings that are normally outside the purview of mainstream literature.

Even otherwise respected authors such as Fritz Springmeier (in *Bloodlines of the Illuminati*) have fallen into this trap, claiming that the Order of the Knights of the Helmet..."was an illuminated secret society with Francis Bacon at its head".

He correctly cites the incident at Gray's Inn (see Part 1), but superimposes the fallacy that this play was a vehicle "to hide its Masonic rituals".

Who is Springmeier's "authority" for coming to this conclusion? None other than Masonic author Alfred Dodd, who Springmeier says is "the best biographer of Francis Bacon". Springmeier further quotes Dodd, who speculates that "Sir Francis Bacon was initiated into a large number of secret occult societies when he was on the continent in Europe".

Springmeier, in relying on secondary, undocumented sources also mistakenly states that "The Queen of England sent Sir Francis Bacon as a young man in his twenties to the continent of Europe", where he supposedly visited a host of countries, including audiences with a number of royal courts.

The reality is that young Francis was sent to Paris with his older brother Anthony as a boy 15 (returning at age 18) in the company of Sir Amias Paulet, the new ambassador to France. The travelling throughout Europe was done later by his older brother Anthony.

Another book which embraces the myth of Francis Bacon and his Knights of the Helmet in Chapter Ten is *The Secret of the Illuminati* by Elizabeth Van Buren, published in 1982.

She states that "In the seventeenth century in Great Britain Sir Francis Bacon formed an *illuminated* Brotherhood called the 'Knights of the Helmet', which was dedicated to Pallas Athena". Her source? None other than Peter Dawkins, Rosicrucian/Baconian apologist and favourite of David Bay.

Dawkins waxes eloquent on the legend of Pallas-Athena and further speculates that "Francis Bacon was known to his contemporaries, including King James, as Apollo".

See http://www.fbrt.org.uk/pages/apollo/descriptions/description-apollo.html.

In this article entitled *Apollo*, Dawkins' starting point is a "woodblock illustration on page 34 of Henry Peacham's book of emblems entitled *Minerva Britanna*, published in London in 1612". "The page is dedicated 'To the most judicious, and learned, Sir Francis Bacon, Knight', and bears the motto 'Ex malis moribus bona leges'" (Out of the death of evil, a legacy of good).

PLATE VI. Emblem dedicated to "the most judicious, and learned, Sir Francis Bacon, Knight." From *Minerva Britannia*, published by Henry Peacham in 1612.

Part 2 – Masonic Deception Regarding Francis Bacon and his Knights of the Helmet

Dawkins then quotes and comments on the woodblock illustration, which has to do with a shepherd piercing a viper with a spear. Similar to David Bay, he then uses this illustration as a basis for all manner of conjecture...conjuring up images of "Bardic mysteries", "Merlin", "the Rose Cross Knight", "the great god Pan", etc. etc.

The easy thing would be to just write this flight of fantasy on Dawkins' part off, except that this woodcut is also pictured on http://www.sirbacon.org/gallery/minerva.html, along with an excerpt from *Bacon Masonry* by Masonic author George Tudhope, which reads in part: "The emblem shows Bacon's direct connection with the Knights of the Helmet from which Freemasonry evolved. The Knight is wearing a high hat which simulates the Knight's Helmet and the Mason's high hat, to indicate his order and invisibility; and he has the staff in his right hand in the act of destroying the Serpent of Ignorance".

As has been pointed out in Part 1 of this rebuttal, "the very structure of Rosicrucianism and Freemasonry is built on a foundation of myth, concealment, fantasy, deception, deviance and perversion", a fact which is admitted to by many high-level Masons such as Manley P. Hall and Albert Pike. The conclusion by Tudhope that the above-noted woodcut emblem "shows Bacon's direct connection with the Knights of the Helmet" is a case in point, specifically in the matter of concealment and deception.

First of all, the quotation from Tudhope's book *Bacon Masonry* cited on the "sirbacon" webpage noted above, conceals pertinent information by omitting part of the two paragraphs quoted, and not indicating that they have done so by using three consecutive periods where the words have been omitted.

Following is the omitted sentence: "This (Peacham's) book (Minerva Britanna) contained a series of devices or emblems, each with a dedication to some noble or distinguished person".

PLATE VI. Emblem dedicated to "the most judicious, and learned, Sir Francis Bacon, Knight." From *Minerva Britannia*, published by Henry Peacham in 1612.

This book contained a series of devices or emblems, each with a dedication to some noble or distinguished person.

The emblem shows Bacon's direct connection with the Knights of the Helmet, from which Freemasonry evolved. The knight is wearing a high hat, which simulates the Knight's Helmet and the Mason's high hat, to indicate his order and his invisibility; and he has the staff in his right hand in the act of destroying the Serpent of Ignorance.

11

Part 2 – Masonic Deception Regarding Francis Bacon and his Knights of the Helmet

This omission is significant for the following reasons:

1. Woodcut emblems recognizing other "Knights" were quite common, and are contained in other emblem books of the day such as *A Choice of Emblemes* by Geffrey Whitney (Leyden, 1586). See pp. 43, 46, 47, 193, 194 and 195.

2. The term "Knight" simply referred to the preferment of knighthood having been granted to an individual, designated by the title *Sir* before his name. This preferment was granted quite liberally during Bacon's time, a fact which caused Bacon to request that his knighthood be conferred in a special ceremony just for him - something which was turned down, much to his chagrin. We are told that "Francis Bacon was dubbed Sir Francis Bacon on 23 July 1603 in the Royal Garden at Whitehall, to mark James' coronation. Three hundred others received the same honour." Perhaps Bacon consoled himself with 'some little physic' (opium), something he was wont to do.

Secondly, the quotation from Tudhope's book deceives the reader by stating in part that "the Knight is wearing a high hat which simulates the Knight's Helmet and the Mason's high hat". The undiscerning reader, having previously been deceived into accepting the "truth" of "Bacon's direct connection with the Knights of the Helmet from which Freemasonry evolved" is now deceived again by the shortened, capitalized term "Knight's Helmet" and by the connection to the "Mason's high hat" on the shepherd (supposedly representing Bacon) in the woodcut emblem.

This brings us to another omission on the "sirbacon" webpage and Tudhope's *Bacon Masonry,* involving the woodcut emblem from page 34 of *Minerva Britanna* by Henry Peacham.

What we aren't told is that Henry Peacham wrote a number of other earlier Emblem books, three of which were dedicated to King James' eldest son Prince Henry, and which were adapted from King James' own emblem book entitled *Basilikon Doron.*

Peacham "followed the tripartite division of James' book"…"the first instructing the prince in his duty towards God; the second in his duty when he should be King; and the third informing him how to behave himself in different things…"

Therefore, in Peacham's first book (dedicated to Prince Henry) "one finds admonitions to love God, to have faith, to read the scriptures with a sanctified heart and to keep a clean conscience". In Peacham's second book, "the emblems largely concern topics such as the Prince's duty to teach his subjects by example, to treat all other princes as brothers and to be liberal to his soldiers. In the third book, "the emblems concern more general principles of behaviour such as avoidance of gluttony, the practice of temperance and moderation in dress, the ignoring of one's dreams, and the cultivation of the equestrian arts".

Part 2 – Masonic Deception Regarding Francis Bacon and his Knights of the Helmet

Peacham's approach was "to place a quotation for King James's *Basilikon Doron* at the foot of each page. Above this, he provided at the head of the page a Latin motto, below which, in the format most used for emblems, was first a picture and then an epigram".

"Peacham often included quotations from the Bible, the Church Fathers, or the Classics, sometimes adding marginalia from similar sources to comment on either the epigram or the motto."

The above three paragraphs are taken from information in the introduction to *The English Emblem Tradition: Henry Peacham's Manuscript Emblem Books*. Edited by Alan R. Young. University of Toronto Press, 1998.

The purpose in introducing Peacham's earlier emblem books, along with the background information, is to put the woodcut emblem from page 34 of Minerva Britanna in its proper context, as follows:

A similar picture, motto and epigram can be found in the Rawlinson Manuscript (Peacham's Book One), the Harleian manuscript (Book Two) and the Royal manuscript (Book Three). What Tudhope speculates as being "a Knight wearing a high hat" is described by Peacham, the author of both *Minerva Britanna* and the three earlier works, as being (1) "a man holding a two-pronged stick. On one prong is impaled a snake", (2) "a man holding a long pointed stick. On the point is impaled a snake", and (3) "a shepherd in a brown hat, red jacket, and blue breeches impales a blue snake with his crook".

Conclusion:

David Bay does a great disservice to his Christian readership by using Rosicrucians and Freemasons to attack the King James Version. In doing this, he is guilty of the same unsavory behaviour and methodology of his new-found "friends". At the very least, David Bay is a double-mined man...even having the gall to title his vilifications against the King James Version as "Defending the King James Version".

"A double minded man is unstable in all his ways." James 1:8 (KJV)

Part 3 – An Introduction to the Matter of Symbols

David Bay, in announcing the posting of his "last article in the 'Defending the KJV' section", summarized the reasons for his ill-advised, ill-conceived and spurious attacks as follows:

1. "to reveal the historic truth of the original KJV"
2. "to go public with some of what we had discovered after radicals had attacked this ministry and our fundamental integrity", and
3. "to open the door to this historical truth (so that) people who love the KJV (can begin) to debate the issues raised by our revelations of the truth".

He concluded his self-congratulatory benediction by announcing that "an official of the Southwest Bible Church called to tell me that he had verified from a computer scanned copy of the original 1611 KJV – whose original was in the Library of Congress—that what we revealed is absolutely correct".

David Bay, as is plainly evident in his weekly headline news commentaries on www.cuttingedge.org, relishes the role of sensationalist. Seemingly every significant political, religious, climatic and scientific event that is reported in the international press is spun into David's latest installment of "As The World Turns".

Not content with the present and future, David has recently produced the first installment of his new DVD series on *The Secret Mysteries of America's Beginnings* for those uninitiated into Rosicrucian and Masonic lore, the same Rosicrucian and Masonic lore that also forms the basis for his sensational attack on the King James Version.

David Bay isn't shy about using the word "truth" to describe "his discoveries". Sadly, we can't even get past the reasons he states for his attacks before encountering one lie after the other. Consider the following points regarding the above-noted reasons:

1. The so-called historic truth (regarding Francis Bacon, the Knights of the Helmet and the symbols) of the original KJV is nothing of the sort. Part 1 and 2 of this rebuttal deal with the matter of Francis Bacon and his so-called Knights of the Helmet as being attributed to nothing more than a performance at Gray's Inn during the Christmas holidays of 1594-95 in London. Part 4 and the subsequent parts will deal with the accusations of the symbols being "occultic and Rosicrucian".

2. David Bay is giving the false impression that he and his ministry have discovered "the historical truth of the original KJV" (regarding Francis Bacon, the Knights of the Helmet and the symbols). Again, this is refuted in part 1 of this rebuttal. The fact of the matter is that many leading Rosicrucians, Freemasons and Baconians, and some Catholics, are on record with these false accusations. Two of these mentioned are Manley P. Hall (1929) and William T. Smedley (in 1910).

3. Again, similar to point 2 above, how can David Bay, with any "fundamental integrity" (his words) say that he is opening this door (to Rosicrucian lore and Masonic myth, not historical truth) when others have already done so a century ago?

I conclude, based on the above considerations, that David Bay had best leave "revelations of the truth" to the Lord Jesus Christ, as He has so perfectly done for us in the scriptures.

As an aside, I find it interesting that David's three "travelling companions" in his attack on the King James Version all have the "R.C." moniker...the Reformed Church (Calvinists), the Rosicrucians and the Roman Catholics.

Lest David be tempted to quote Amos 3:7 (Surely the Lord God will do nothing, but he revealeth his secret unto his servants the prophets), it would be prudent that he first consider Amos 3:3 (Can two walk together, except they be agreed?). Agreeing to walk together with not one, but three, proven King James Version despisers, certainly "reveals" what David really believes with regard to the authority and veracity of the KJV.

"And have no fellowship with the unfruitful works of darkness, but rather reprove them. For it is a shame even to speak of those things which are done of them in secret. But all things that are reproved are made manifest by the light: for whatsoever doth make manifest is light". (Ephesians 5:11-13 KJV).

To conclude this section on "Bay's benediction", quoting from "the official" who scanned the 1611 KJV **only** acts to confirm that what David has is a reproduction of the 1611 KJV, **not** "that what (he) revealed is absolutely correct", as David so naively (or deceptively) claims.

To move on to the matter of symbols, it is important to realize that this a subject which is as old as civilization itself, a subject which is complex and highly specialized, and a subject about which many of the primary reference books are quite rare and expensive, or impossible to obtain at any price.

Sadly, David has not aided his already-tarnished credibility by citing a paltry number of mass-market secondary sources, heavily biased sources (occultists, Rosicrucians, Freemasons, Baconians, and the like), and others with an axe to grind alongside David's "cutting edge".

Part 3 – An Introduction to the Matter of Symbols

Bay (the pretender) has even gone so far as to do a "hatchet job" on the good work of real defenders of the King James Version such as Texe Marrs by misrepresenting portions of his new book *Codex Magica*.

We'll start off with some background information, a few points which, of necessity, are brought forward from the previous parts of this rebuttal.

1. Despite the pretentious claims of many writers, the weight of evidence (which is borne out by dictionaries such as *Wikipedia,* along with Rosicrucian and Masonic authorities) is that Rosicrucianism (which preceded Freemasonry) can only be traced as a formal, organized group to 1614, when its first writings were published. Other claims of an earlier origin are based on unreliable sources, myth, speculation or wishful thinking.

2. The influence of Francis Bacon in the court of King James I, especially prior to the publication of the 1611 KJV, is shown to be quite minor according to the latest scholarly work entitled *Hostage to Fortune: The Troubled Life of Francis Bacon.* Since "the gloves are off", judging by the vileness of Bay's attack, we should mention at this point that Bacon is very fortunate indeed that he wasn't beheaded, a fate that befell other sodomites of his day. Even though his mother was aware of this predilection on the part of Francis and his older brother Anthony, this correspondence, and that of others touching on this subject, apparently did not reach the ears of the King. Other problems, however, did lead to Bacon's eventual disgrace.

3. Woodcuts, which were common in books from the early 16th century to the late 17th century, were ornamental devices carved from wood blocks by craftsmen. These ornamental devices, which included both emblems and symbols, served as borders, head and tail pieces, title pages, decorative letters and pictorial illustrations of the text.

Head Piece >>

Tail Piece >>

Ornamental Borders >>

In some cases, an artist would prepare the illustrations on paper, the engraver would transfer them to wood blocks, and these wood blocks would be made available (sold or rented) to a printer or publisher. In other cases, the artist and engraver would be the same person. These wood blocks were usually done initially as a set, or series, for a particular book...which might, due to popularity, be published in many editions and printings. Due to the painstaking nature, and therefore relatively high cost, of preparing the more elaborate woodcuts, they were shared by many publishers, frequently spanning decades of use. This "sharing" of woodcuts was not necessarily confined to a particular genre of books, although it goes without saying that the subject matter of some (eg. religious scenes) confined their use to certain books, while other emblemata such as animals, fleurons, and the like could be used anywhere. For example, Guillaume Borluyt, after he studied law, traveled throughout France, and found himself short of money when he arrived in Lyons in 1557. There he met the publisher Jean de Tournes, who asked Borluyt to prepare Flemish verses to a series of woodcuts he had in his possession. These consisted of illustrations on the Old and New Testament by Bernard Salomon (c. 1506 - c. 1561), arguably the foremost woodcut artist of his day.

The Old Testament series, consisting of 199 woodcuts, was first published in 1553. Salomon completed the set in 1555, and the New Testament series, consisting of 96 woodcuts, was also published in 1553 with French texts, and in 1557 with Dutch texts. Salomon's woodcut series of Bible text illustrations continued to be popular, and was used in Bibles of many languages throughout continental Europe, eventually finding their way to the English publishing house of the Barkers, and thence into later reprints of the 1611 King James Version.

The above information was gleaned in part from a biographical note in French pasted on the first fly-leaf of the *Dutch Verses to a Famous Biblical Woodcut Series by Bernard Salomon,* authored by the above-noted Guillaume Borluyt. The market price for this extremely rare book is approx. US$16,000. This serves to illustrate my point about the primary reference books being quite rare and expensive.

4.   Copperplates were another type of ornamental device, commonly found on title pages of Bibles and other major works. The general title page (frontispiece) of the 1611 KJV was prepared by the Flemish engraver Cornelis Boel (c. 1576 – 1621), who was working in England at the time. Boel had previously engraved plates for works by Otto van Veen (1556-1629) in Antwerp, and later went on to produce portraits of kings and important persons in Flanders, and finally established himself in Spain, engraving title pages and other portraits for leading personages there.

5. The genealogy pages of the 1611 KJV were designed by John Speed (1552-1629), who was noted for his work on atlases of the day.

6. One of the many difficulties in attributing meanings to symbols is that meanings change over time, sometimes from culture to culture, and are subject to manipulation or perversion for various reasons, as we shall see. The symbols used in books published throughout mainland Europe and the British Isles during the 16th and 17th centuries came from a variety of sources, some ancient and some more recent, and were incorporated into various woodcuts and copperplates, in books of all genres. Symbols, unlike emblems, were not in most cases printed with explanatory mottos, epigrams, poems or other references to indicate their origin and meaning. In the case of emblems, these explanatory passages came in different modes such as didactic (instructive), documentary, explicative, narrative, moralistic and aesthetic...making it apparent to the informed reader if future authors citing these emblems were engaged in manipulation or perversion.

    Sadly, David Bay and his Rosicrucian-Masonic-Baconian travelling companions have done just that, in perverting the meaning of an emblem from page 34 of Henry Peacham's *Minerva Britanna*. This is dealt with in Part 2 – Masonic Deception Regarding Francis Bacon and his Knights of the Helmet. My question at this juncture is... If David Bay and his Rosicrucian sources cannot get the meaning of an emblem right when the meaning is given to them as part of the emblematic structure, how can they be trusted to interpret symbols?

    Whether the problem is incompetence or deception, the result is the same. David Bay and his travelling companions have about as much credibility as the Wizard of Oz engaged in his antics behind the curtain.

7. The field of emblem literature and symbols is not only complex, but broad in its scope. A sampling of the 16th and 17th century embematists, whose works have been consulted from the author's library for this rebuttal, include Andreas Alciatus, Horozco Covaruvius, Cesare Ripa, Jan Van Der Noot, Florentinus Schoonhovius, Jean Jacques Boissart, Otto van Veen, Paolo Giovio, Andrew Willet, Thomas Combe, Bernard Salomon, Claude Paradin, Hans Holbein the Younger, George Wither, Geffrey Whitney, Francis Quarles, Johann Reuchlin, Henry Peacham, Christopher Plantin, Symeoni, Joannes Sambucus, Gilles Corrozet, Guillaume de La Pierrere and Horapollo Niliacus. Many Rosicrucian and Baconian books, as well as websites such as www.sirbacon.org have also been consulted.

8. The "father" of European emblem writing is generally considered to be Andreas Alciatus (or Andrea Alciati), who was an Italian lawyer. His first emblem book, *Emblematum Liber*, was published in Italy in 1531. According to Professor Mario Praz, Alciatus is credited with establishing both the form and name of the emblem. Dozens of emblematists followed suit from various countries throughout Europe, with Geffrey Whitney being the first English writer with his work *A Choice of Emblemes*, published in Leyden, in 1586.

    Until Whitney's *Emblemes*, printers and publishers in England such as Christopher Barker, Richard Field, John Day, and Richard Pynson had to use woodcuts and copperplates from printers in Continental Europe. The first copperplate illustration found in an English book was in the 1540 publication *The Byrth of Mankynde*, a book on midwifery.

9. From the middle of the 16th century to the end of the 17th century, emblem books took on a distinct literary form. "This consisted of a collection of pictures…each accompanied by a motto and moral exposition usually in verse. In seventeenth century terminology it was generally the picture alone that was the Emblem, the motto was called the 'Word', and the poet added verses or 'moralised the emblem'". "These explanatory poems were often designated *The Meaning of the Emblem*, or *The Mind of the Frontispiece.*" (Rosemary Fleming, *English Emblem Books*. London. 1948)

    During this period it became common to select single emblems, or a series of emblems, often without text from works already published and use them to illustrate frontispieces (title pages). These emblems would adorn the "architecture" of the frontispiece, which could be a full-page woodcut or a print from a copperplate engraving. Their purpose was to give the reader an indication of the book's subject matter. In order to understand the "meaning of the emblem" or "the mind of the frontispiece", therefore, one had accept it *prima facie* at, or for, the time it was printed.

    It is important to realize, and accept, that there was no malicious or devious intent on the part of the printers to trick, or fool, the reader with this use of emblems or symbols. To put it another way, these emblems and symbols were "an aid to reflection, not a means of deception". This tactic came into use later with groups such as the Rosicruciams and Freemasons. An example of this tactic, which David Bay has fallen for, is the superimposing of the compass and rose/cross over the emblem of the "pelican in her piety", which he covers in his first article. This will be dealt with later as part of this rebuttal.

10. It is important to understand the difference in meaning between emblems and symbols. EMBLEMS equate picture with meaning in an extrinsic, or known sense. This can be done explicitly, through the use of poems, epigrams, etc. or implicitly, as in the case of "the pelican in her piety", through the established meaning of the emblem in the culture. "The image remains independent of the ideas it conveys, and does not wholly embody them." In emblems, there is an "imposition of meaning upon a predetermined image. Each detail in them is a pictorial detail, to be seen by the eye", which leads to an image which is objective, fixed and definite. Rosemary Freeman, who is quoted in this paragraph, gives this example from George Withers' *A Collection of Emblemes* (1635) p.109, where he writes about the marigold (which was an interchangeable term with the sunflower at that time).

> When, with a serious musing, I behold
> The gratefull, and obsequious *Marigold*,
> How duely, ev'ry morning, she displayes
> Her open brest, when *Titan* spreads his Rayes.
> How she observes him in his daily walke,
> Still bending towards him, her tender stalke;
> How, when he downe declines, she droopes and mournes,
> Bedew'd (as 'twere) with teares, till he returnes.

11. SYMBOLS, on the other hand, invest meaning in the image or picture through identification rather than equation. The meaning is intrinsic, occult (in the sense of being hidden) and natural. Ideas within the meaning of the picture are developed, expanded and interpreted. Symbols encompass imagination and experience, and are thus subjective, elastic and variable. Freeman gives us an example from William Blake's *Songs of Experience* (1794) of the marigold/sunflower as a symbol.

> Ah, Sun-flower! weary of time,
> Who countest the steps of the Sun,
> Seeking after that sweet golden clime
> Where the traveller's journey is done:
>
> Where the Youth pined away with desire,
> And the pale Virgin shrouded in snow
> Arise from their graves, and aspire
> Where my Sun-flower wishes to go.

Part 3 – An Introduction to the Matter of Symbols

Henry Estienne maintained that there were four branches of symbolical writing: enigma, emblem, fable and parable. Whitney describes his emblems as being of three kinds: historical, natural and moral. From the above information, hopefully the reader can see that emblems and symbols, although closely connected, are not the same thing.

Much has been written about the development and use of emblems and symbols in books published during the sixteenth and seventeenth centuries. The above information is a thumbnail sketch, if even that, of this broad and complex subject. Much other information pertinent to the matter at hand could be given, such as the personification of virtues as a common theme, not only in emblem books, but in their use on frontispieces, headpieces, tailpieces and ornamental borders in books of all genres. Common themes on the subject of personification of virtues include the nine worthies, the four seasons, the four elements, the five senses and the three theological virtues. The remaining background information pertinent to David Bay's accusations and claims regarding occult (in the sense of magical, mysterious, evil) symbols in the 1611 and 1619 KJV bibles will be included as part of the rebuttal to each of his accusations.

As has been stated previously, David Bay, for his own reasons, has chosen to "join hands" with Rosicrucian and Masonic writers, among others, in order to launch this latest attack on the King James Version. He is favourably quoting these writers, who are purveyors of deception and adepts of arcana, in this attack that he has called a defence. What a tangled web of deceit David has woven. It reminds me of the words penned by another emblem writer, Francis Quarles, from his *Emblems, Divine and Moral*:

> A world of dangers, and a world of snares:
> The close Pursuers busie hands do plant
> Snares in thy substance; Snares attend thy want;
> Snares in thy credit; Snares in thy Disgrace;
> Snares in thy high estate; Snares in thy base;
> Snares tuck thy bed; and Snares around thy boord;
> Snares watch thy thoughts; and snares attach thy word;
> Snares in thy quiet; Snares in thy commotion;
> Snares in thy diet; Snares in thy devotion;
> Snares lurk in thy resolves; Snares, in thy doubt;
> Snares lie within thy heart, and Snares, without
> Snares are above thy head, and Snares, beneath;
> Snares in thy sicknesse; Snares are in thy death.

Who would have thought that someone like David Bay would be setting all these snares for the believer?

Part 4 – The Accuser Speaks: A Summary of David Bay's Claims Against the KJV

Although the Introduction, Part 1 and Part 2 of this rebuttal deal with David Bay's claim that Francis Bacon, the Knights of the Helmet and even King James I himself placed their "Kabbalistic, Rosicrucian, Masonic, occult" seal on the 1611 and 1619 KJV, or words to that effect repeated mantra-like throughout his five Cutting Edge articles, more information will be brought to light in this part, and succeeding parts to refute this ridiculous claim.

Following is a summary of David Bay's other claims, in the order they will be dealt with.

1. "The KJV title page is a typical Rosicrucian scene and it outlines the traditional belief as to the various stages which a Perfected Kabbalist Man can achieve immortality."
   From Article 1001, page 4.

2. The "Hebraic letters at the very top center (of the KJV title page) have been identified by an orthodox Jewish scholar as the Kabbalistic Tetragrammaton", and "no orthodox Jewish priest would ever write God's name like this…it was…clearly occultic".
   From Article 1001, page 4-5.

3. "The lower hem of the garment worn by the High Priest (KJV title page) has symbols filling up this space (that) are Luciferic All-Seeing Eyes."   Article 1001, page 5-6.

4. The KJV title page depicts a "swan with young brood pecking her breast", part of the "five steps to immortality according to Rosicrucianism."   Article 1001, page 6-7.

5. The KJV title page depicts a "Satanic Phoenix Bird…holding an ink well up to the Perfected Man on the right in the Lower World"
   Article 1001, page 8-9.

6. The KJV title page depicts a "man (in the Celestial/Middle World) with the X", X being "the sign of Osiris, the great Egyptian sun god", "the Chaldean sky god: the (ancient) solar god", etc.
   Article 1001, page 9-11.

7. The "upper portion of 'page lii' in the 1611 KJV Bible" contains "dozens and dozens of Masonic Handshakes, proving once again our contention that Sir Francis Bacon – the consummate Kabbalist Master of his day – had his hands on the Bible".
   Article 1001, page 12 and Article 1002.

8. Pan, "the Greek god of sexual lust and orgies is depicted prominently twice in the original 1611 KJV Bible." - Article 1003.

9. "The (Baphomet) Goatshead/Devil's Head banner (along with a 6-6-6 representation) is in the 1611 and 1619 KJV Bibles, (because) Sir Francis Bacon, King James I, and the Knights of the Helmet (planned) to produce a Rosicrucian Mystic Bible".
Article 1004, page 1-4.

10. "The figure of Neptune (representing Satan) astride his horse and lifting his trident high is the woodcut for the first letter 'T' appearing on the title page of the Gospel of Matthew, 1611 KJV, page 1143".
Article 1004, page 5-6.

11. There is a "demonic bat-like creature in the middle of the letter 'G' in the woodcut at the beginning of the Book to the Hebrews, in the 1611 KJV edition".
Article 1004, page 6.

12. "The famous Rosicrucian-Baconian banner" called "Light A - Dark A" (the signature of Francis Bacon and the Knights of the Helmet) appears "in the 1619 KJV, at the bottom of the Genealogies page".
Article 1004, page 7.

13. "Sir Francis Bacon and his Knights of the Helmet spent part of the year…re-arranging the Bible so that its very structure formed two pillars – from Genesis 1 to Revelation 22 – with the mystical number '33' in the middle". This was done under the approving eye of King James, who "was a Rosicrucian and Freemason himself".

As noted above, there is more that can and will be said with respect to David Bay's claim that Francis Bacon, his Knights of the Helmet and even King James himself (all allegedly members of a secret cabal of Kabbalists and Rosicrucians) placed occult (in the sense of magical, mystical) symbols on the title pages, woodcuts and genealogy pages of the 1611 and 1619 KJV Bibles.

David, as self-appointed guide for this magical mystery tour, welcomes one and all to come aboard as he and his friends hand out Rose-Coloured glasses in order that we may see what they see…a "spirit world" comprised of a "Lower World", a "Celestial World" and a "Super-Celestial World".

Sadly, I can't compete with the pizzazz of these carnival-like enticements and grandiose claims. The reader will have to be content with the tedium of reality, facts, documentation and scholarship.

Part 4 – The Accuser Speaks: A Summary of David Bay's Claims Against the KJV

For example, let's consider the latest scholarly work on the development of the King James Bible, entitled *A Textual History of the King James Bible* by David Norton (2005), published by Cambridge University Press. Contrary to the unfounded claims of David Bay, consider the following conclusions reached by Norton (pp. 27-28) based on the extant evidence:

1. "Six companies produced draft translations between 1604 and 1608."

2. "The work was called in in 1608, and the companies forwarded it to the general meeting in the form of annotations to the Bishop's Bible text. The general meeting had working copies made of some of the submitted work…"

3. "It worked over these in small groups in 1609 and 1610, producing as final copy a heavily annotated and interleaved Bishop's Bible."

4. "John Bois's notes give a glimpse of the work done in 1610."

5. "In 1610 and 1611, two men* worked over the whole text in co-operation with the printer, establishing the KJB as first printed in 1611. Whatever manuscripts there might have been, this, with the second printing, effectively became the master copy of the KJB."

   * The "two men" in question, as Norton points out a few pages earlier, were Dr. Miles Smith, Bishop of Gloucester and Dr. Thomas Bilson, Bishop of Winchester. This information is gleaned from a 1611 work authored by A.W. Pollard.

The point of citing these conclusions reached by Norton is that there is no credible evidence that anyone has come forward with to prove that Francis Bacon, his (imaginary) Knights of the Helmet or King James himself had any influence in the translating or printing of the King James Version.

This includes the title page, woodcuts, genealogy pages and other ornamental devices.

Let's now examine **Claim #1** above, namely that **"the KJV title page is a typical Rosicrucian scene and it outlines the traditional belief as to the various stages through which a Perfected Kabbalist Man can achieve immortality."**

After one gets over his or her "Say what?" initial reaction, and realizes that Bay is serious about his view of the title page as depicting the "Rosicrucian worldview", a rebuttal to this fantastic claim is required. Consider the following points in response to Bay's statements on this matter.

Part 4 – The Accuser Speaks: A Summary of David Bay's Claims Against the KJV

1. Bay quotes from *The Rosicrucian Enlightenment*. There are at least two problems here. Firstly, Bay spells both the author's first and last name incorrectly. He cites the author as Francis Yeats. He is so absorbed with Francis Bacon that he doesn't seem to realize that the author is a woman, which usually means that her first name would have to be spelled as "Frances". Her last name, unlike that of W.B. Yeats, is spelled "Yates". Dame Frances Amelia Yates, a prolific author on secret societies and arcana, was born in 1899 and died in 2001. This is not a good start for David.

    Secondly, Bay is as aware of the latest scholarship in the field of esotericism as he is about the best price on a facsimile reprint of the 1611 KJV. The $400.00 he could have saved on his KJV would have more than covered the price, including shipping and handling, on the recently published (2005) two volume *Dictionary of Gnosis and Western Esotericism*.

    The book description informs us that "this is the first comprehensive reference work to cover the entire domain of 'Gnosis and Western Esotericism' from the period of Late Antiquity to the present". There are "around 400 articles by over 180 international specialists", the work is 1258 pages and is published by the renowned Brill Academic Publishers (March 8, 2005). Bart D. Ehrman, James A. Gray Distinguished Professor and Chair of Religious Studies, University of North Carolina at Chapel Hill describes this work as "brilliantly conceived", "skilfully executed", "detailed and insightful" and "produced by an impressive array of renowned scholars". High praise indeed!

    The point in bringing this new work to Bay's attention (and to the attention of those who "take Yates at her word") is that this new reference work points out some deficiencies in Yates's conclusions on "the development of hermetic philosophy and related traditions such as the 'Christian kabbalah' and the Rosicrucian furor of the early 17th century".

    The following cautionary note is given: "While Yates's work has been of the greatest importance in bringing these subjects to the attention of a wide audience, particularly in the anglophone world, her grand narrative of 'the Hermetic Tradition' as a coherent and quasi- autonomous counterculture based upon magic and leading to science has been called into question by subsequent research."

2. As is the case with Bay's fixation on Francis Bacon, his fixation on Rosicrucian lore lands him into his next quagmire. What standard reference works** would term as a typical frontispiece or title page format, David Bay sees as "a typical Rosicrucian scene". Neither the sentences cited from Yates's work nor the follow-up sentences cited from the Rose Cross Magazine link the KJV title page to a Rosicrucian worldview, but Bay doesn't seem to allow facts or logic to deter him.

Part 4 – The Accuser Speaks: A Summary of David Bay's Claims Against the KJV

**

- A History of the Art of Printing. Henry Noel Humphreys. London. 1867.
- Art of the Printed Book, 1455-1955: Masterpieces of Typography Through Five Centuries from the Collections of the Pierpont Morgan Library. 1973.
- The Comely Frontispiece. Margery Corbett and R.W. Lightbown. London. 1979.
- Engraving in England in the Sixteenth & Seventeenth Centuries. Arthur M. Hind. Cambridge University Press. 1955.

Leaving the obvious view regarding the title page format aside for the moment, one has to ask why Bay would come to the conclusion that the "three stages of existence" supposedly depicted would "accurately reflect...Rosicrucian thinking"? Why not any of the following religions, which have the same "three stages of existence", such as Mormonism (telestial, terrestrial and celestial) OR Swedenborg's vision (natural, spiritual and celestial) OR the Goth vision of the Lower World (the underworld), the Middle World (the Earth) and the Upper World (the Celestial Courts)?

Part of the answer to this question may be that Bay has travelled this route at least twice before in articles from the late nineties regarding the "ten nation" map of the world as originally envisioned by the Club of Rome and another on N.A.F.T.A. This "Rosicrucian worldview" and "three stages of existence" were linked to articles on these political-economic entities. None of these linkages make any sense unless you are David Bay.

Part and parcel of the "Rosicrucian three stages of existence", depicted on the KJV title page according to David, is the achievement of immortality by the "Perfected Kabbalist Man". As is the case with the "three stages of existence", however, the "Perfected Man" is not a teaching exclusive to Rosicrucianism or Kabbalism. The following belief systems incorporate this concept of the Perfected Man: Epicurianism, Stoicism, neo-Platonism, Gnosticism, Theosophy, Confucianism, Hinduism, Buddhism, Mormonism, Christian Science, Islam, Urantia, et al. It is obvious, though, that the term "Perfected neo-Platonic Man", or "Perfected Buddhist Man", or "Perfected Islamic Man" just doesn't have the same ring!

One might also ask, why stop at three stages of existence? Heinrich Cornelius Agrippa, in his *Three Books of Occult Philosophy*, published in 1651, claims that there are six worlds: the Infernall soul, the lesser world, the Elementary world, the Celestiall world, the Intellectuall world, and the exemplary world. Then again, why not just play the Game Boy video game *Final Fantasy Legend II*, where "the player visits twelve distinct worlds, in addition to the Celestial world and the Shrine at its center"?

Beauty (or fantasy in this case) is in the eye of the beholder.

3. Now that we have dealt with David's chutzpah, perhaps we can come back to our present world. There is really nothing difficult or mysterious about title pages or frontispieces of the sixteenth and seventeenth centuries. Various emblems or symbols (or both) are arranged around an architectural façade in order to illustrate to the prospective reader what is behind this façade, or what comes after the title page.

It is common, due to the fact that this façade can be traced back to Greek and Roman architecture, that three components or elements are commonly portrayed:
   (i)   the foundation, base or plinth
   (ii)   the main structure, with or without separate columns and
   (iii)   the roof, which may consist of an architrave (plain or decorated lintel), a freize (sculptured border above the lintel), a cornice (fascia/overhang), and a pediment (decorative/sculptured gable - rectangle, triangle or other geometric shape).

Examples of these architectural facades which served as patterns for sixteenth and seventeenth century frontispieces are:

   •   The Façade of the Treasury of the Siphnians in the Sanctuary of Apollo at Delphi. c. 530 B.C.
   •   The Ara Pacis in Rome.   Constructed from 13-9 B.C.
   •   Pierre Lescot's Square Court of the Louvre in Paris.   Begun in 1546 A.D.

Examples of frontispieces with a format similar to that of the 1611 KJV title page are:

   (i)   Frontispiece for *The Theatre of the Empire of Great Britain*. London. 1611. John Speed, Printer.
   (ii)   Frontispiece for *The Holy Bible Containing the Old Testament and the New*. London. 1708. (Anon.)
   (iii)   Frontispiece for *Fasciculus Geographicus*. Cologne. 1608. Matthias Quad, Printer.
   (iv)   Frontispiece for *De Touts Les Pais-Bas*. Antwerp. 1582. Christopher Plantin, Printer.
   (v)   Frontispiece for *Italiae, Sclavonia, et Graeciae*. Amsterdam. c.1610. Gerard Mercator, Printer.
   (vi)   Frontispiece for *Theatrum Orbis Terrarum*. Amsterdam. 1635. Willem and Joanne Blaeu, Printer.
   (vii)   Frontispiece for *Indiae Orientalis*. Frankfurt. 1601. Jon Huygen van Linschoten, Printer.
   (viii) Frontispiece for *Urbium Praecipvarum Totius Mundi*. Cologne. 1581. George Braun and Franz Hogenberg, Printer.

Part 4 – The Accuser Speaks: A Summary of David Bay's Claims Against the KJV

Did Francis Bacon, the (imaginary) Knights of the Helmet and King James order these "Rosicrucian scenes" of the "three stages of existence" to be placed on these, and hundreds of other frontispieces - on books all over the European continent during the sixteenth and seventeenth centuries?

Who knows? In David Bay's parallel world, seemingly anything is possible.

𝒫𝒶𝓇𝓉 5 – 𝒜 𝓡𝑒𝓈𝓅𝑜𝓃𝓈𝑒 𝓉𝑜 𝒟𝒶𝓋𝒾𝒹 ℬ𝒶𝓎'𝓈 𝒸𝓁𝒶𝒾𝓂

that the "Hebraic letters at the very top center (of the KJV title page) have been identified by an orthodox Jewish scholar as the Kabbalistic Tetragrammaton", and "no orthodox Jewish priest would ever write God's name like this...it was...clearly occultic".
From Article 1001, page 4-5

My response to this claim will be broken down into five sections:

1. Proving one's allegations in a court of law.
2. Defining terms.
3. The Altered (Kabbalistic) Tetragrammaton .
4. The traditional Hebrew Tetragrammaton as represented in the Masoretic pointed text.
5. The traditional Christian meaning of the Dove.

Proving one's allegations in a court of law

There is a well-worn phrase that goes "saying so doesn't make it so". This applies to David's unidentified "orthodox Jewish scholar" as well as his declaration regarding all orthodox Jewish priests. Coupled with his "clearly occultic" mantra, these accusations will be summarily shown to be nothing but more hubris on Bay's part.

In a criminal proceeding, the accuser (plaintiff) must prove his case "beyond a reasonable doubt" to a judge or jury. In a civil proceeding, the plaintiff is required to prove his case on the balance of evidence being in his favour. I'll leave it up to the reader (one of the "jury") to decide whether he or she wants to treat this as a "criminal" matter or "civil" matter.

The onus, either way, is for David to prove his case with regard to the previously summarized claims about Francis Bacon, the Knights of the Helmet, King James I, the format and content of the KJV title page, the woodcuts, and so on. In a court of law, an unidentified so-called "orthodox Jewish scholar" does not classify as a witness. Further, to make a statement such as "no orthodox Jewish priest would ever write…" would be thrown out by a judge as an unsubstantiated claim. In other words, there is no credible evidence presented to back this up, only pseudo-evidence from "occult" sources, a label that Bay is continually trying to pin on the King James Version. This type of skewed thinking has become a pattern in the Cutting Edge articles.

Part 5 – A Response to David Bay's claim

Defining terms

As noted previously, although emblems and symbols are related, they are not the same thing. It is extremely important, in light of the gravity of Bay's accusations, that the meaning of these words is clearly understood.

As the reader will note, David Bay, either due to ignorance or attempted deception, classifies all the images on the KJV title page and woodcuts as "symbols", but this will be shown not to be the case. In addition to the previous information given in this regard in Part 3, Section 6 through 11, consider the following information quoted from *Literature: Structure, Sound, and Sense* by Laurence Perrine, 4th Edition (1983) New York.

The ability to interpret symbols is nevertheless essential for a full understanding of literature. Beginning readers should be alert for symbolical meanings but should observe the following cautions:

1. The story itself must furnish a clue that a detail is to be taken symbolically…Symbols nearly always signal their existence by emphasis, repetition, or position. In the absence of such signals, we should be reluctant to identify an idea as symbolical.

2. The meaning of a literary symbol must be established and supported by the entire context of the story (or poem). The symbol has its meaning *in* the story, not *outside* it…

3. To be called a symbol, an item must suggest a meaning different in kind from its literal meaning…

4. A symbol may have more than one meaning. It may suggest a cluster of meanings… This is not to say that it can mean anything we want it to: the area of possible meanings is always controlled by the context…The meaning cannot be confined to any one… (quality): it is all of them, and therein lies the symbol's value.

To summarize, an emblem (or image, as Perrine terms it) and a symbol can be difficult to differentiate. Perrine's somewhat simplistic definition is, in part: "An image (emblem) means only what it is…a symbol means what it is and something more too".

The Altered (Kabbalistic) Tetragrammaton

The Altered (Kabbalistic) Tetragrammaton is a central, but concealed, element of the Kabbalistic (Sefirotic) system. Considering the thousands of books, articles and various other writings on the Kabbalah (to receive, accept) and the Tetragrammaton (four letters), it is at best possible to just scratch the surface of this subject matter as it relates to Bay's accusation.

As with Rosicrucianism, the roots of Kabbalism are uncertain, although its elements of Gnosticism, neo-Platonism and Talmudic and Midrashic traditions can be traced back to the early part of the first millennium A.D. Some historians tell us that Babylonian Jewish scholars gradually developed this esoteric, mystical system in the period from 600 – 1000 A.D., and formalized it as the Zohar (Book of Light or Splendor) at around 1300 A.D. after this community of Jewish exiles relocated to various countries in Europe such as Italy, France, Germany and Spain. Others, however, maintain that the Zohar was written by Simeon ben Jochai and first printed in Mantua in 1558. The Zohar is largely mathematical in nature, and incorporates number symbolism called gematria, notarikon and temurah along with magic, anagrams, and the names of angelic beings. The second authoritative book of Kabbalah, called the Sefer Yetzirah (Book of Creation), was supposedly written between 100 B.C. and 800 A.D.

The system of Kabbalah is centered around the Sefirotic Tree of Life, and teaches that the world came into existence from a transcendent "God" through a series of emanations, and that the enlightened man could progress in stages toward "God" through prayer, meditation and magic (as above, so below).

As noted above, even though the Tetragrammaton is a central element of Kabbalah, if one examines the ten Sephira, or emanations of the Sefirotic Tree of Life, one will see that it has been altered from the original, and that the Y-H-V-H (Yod, Hey, Vav, Hey) letter group is not found.

<< 1611 KJV title page: Tetragrammaton

The Traditional Hebrew Tetragrammaton as represented in the Masoretic pointed text

There are three website articles dealing with the traditional Hebrew Tetragrammaton which give evidence to refute David Bay's claim that "no orthodox Jewish priest would ever write God's name like this", referring to the Tetragrammaton at the top of the 1611 KJV title page. One article is by Dr. Thomas M. Strouse, a professor at Emmanuel Baptist Theological Seminary and a member of the Dean Burgon Society. The second article is written by a Calvinist (to show that I am not biased against quoting documented evidence from those of this persuasion) by the name of Scott Jones who, interestingly, references material from Dean Burgon on his website. The third article is written by Jay C. Treat, Ph.D. of the University of Pennsylvania.

Part 5 – A Response to David Bay's claim

Websites articles referenced:
www.lamblion.net/Articles/ScottJones/jehovah1.htm
http://ccat.sas.upenn.edu/rs/2/Judaism/name/
http://www.emmanuel-newington.org/seminary/resources/JHVH.pdf

In addition to these website articles, the reader is encouraged to consult chapter 11 of *In Awe of Thy Word* by Dr. G. A. Riplinger.

After digesting this information regarding the propriety of the Tetragrammaton as represented in the Masoretic pointed text, it would be appropriate to cite other examples of title pages (or frontispieces) which have the identical (ie. complete with vowel points) representation of the 1611 KJV Tetragrammaton.

The final two examples cited lead one to believe that God indeed has a sense of humour...much like the situation of Fredrich Nietzsche, who claimed that "God is dead". Apparently someone, after Nietzsche died, changed the words on his epitaph to read "Nietzsche is dead, God is alive".

Examples of the traditional Hebrew Tetragrammaton with vowel points on various frontispieces and portraitures around the time of the publishing of the early versions of the KJV Bible:

1) Saluste du Barta's *Devine Weekes and Workes*, 1605. Engraved by Christopher Switzer.
2) Jodocus Hondius' *Map of the World in a Roundel*, 1589.
3) William Kip's *Map of the World in a Roundel*, 1602.
4) Hymen Coelestis' *Charles I, as Prince, Standing With the Infanta Maria*.
5) Saluste du Barta's *Devine Weekes and Workes*, 1621. Engraved by Renold Elstrack.
6) Willem Van De Passe's *Portraiture of Frederick V, King of Bohemia, and family*.
7) *Bishop's Bible*, 1602. Artwork: Rowland Lackey. Woodcut: Christopher Switzer.
8) *The Whole Book of Psalmes*, 1623. Pr. by C. Legg, Printer to Cambridge University.
9) Martin Droeshout's title-plate for Helkiah Crooke's *Description of the Body of Man*.
10) Samuel Ward's *To God, In Memory of His Double Deliveraunce*, 1621.

Samuel Ward, one of the King James Version translators, was also an accomplished emblematist (and caricaturist), and did the artwork for this frontispiece. The engraver is anonymous. From the Tetragrammaton, a ray of light reaches the barrels of powder (set in place by Guy Fawkes and his fellow Jesuit conspirators,) where Ward inserted the Latin caption *Video Rideo,* which means "I see and smile".

Last, but not least, we have the traditional Hebrew Tetragrammaton with vowel points on none other than the frontispiece of Francis Bacon's *Sylva Sylvarum or A Naturall Historie In Ten Centuries*, published posthumously by W. Rawley, Doctor of Divinty.*

Part 5 – A Response to David Bay's claim

Frontispiece of Francis Bacon's Sylva Sylvarum

In addition to the aforementioned Tetragrammaton, Rawley put the "signature" of his orthodox Christian beliefs on this title page, and elsewhere, of Bacon's writings in the following ways:

1)   The two cherubim gazing in different directions, the one looking at the Tetragrammaton and the other at the globe below are indicating that the light of God's truth is shining on the *Mundus Intelleactuallis*, the world of human knowledge. This indicates that Rawley, in his capacity as a Doctor of Divinity, was reconciling the new scientific method as expounded by Bacon with the revealed truth of Christian orthodoxy.

2) Rawley indicated his belief that God approved of the advancement of learning through the new scientific method by his use of a quotation from Genesis 1:4, *"Et vidit Deus lucem quod efset bona"* (And God saw the light, that it was good).

3) At the end of his preface to the reader, he states: "I will conclude with an usuall speech of his Lordships. That this work of his *Naturall History*, is the world as God made it; For that it hath nothing of imagination".

* The information on *Sylva Sylvarum* is taken from an article by Pablo Alvarez, Curator of Rare Books at the University of Rochester Department of Rare Books, Special Collections and Preservation. See www.library.rochester.edu/index.cfm?PAGE=3613

The Traditional Christian meaning of the Dove

We conclude this part with a response to David Bay's claim that the dove on the 1611 KJV title page is "the pagan symbol of the Spirit of God".

1611 KJV title page: Dove

As noted previously, David struggles with words and their meanings, which doesn't help in enhancing his credibility with the informed reader. First of all, in labelling the dove as a pagan symbol, he is saying that it is a heathen symbol, especially pertaining to one who worshipped the gods (small "g") of ancient Greece and Rome.**

**The New Lexicon Webster's Encyclopedic Dictionary of the English Language, Canadian Edition (1988)

Part 5 – A Response to David Bay's claim

This definition is obviously incompatible with the capitalized term "Spirit of God".

Further, we again find David making a claim with no evidence to back him up. In other words, saying that the dove is "the pagan symbol of the Spirit of God" is not only unsupportable grammatically, it is unsupportable historically.

Following are examples of the dove symbology in various cultures.***

1. Slavic culture – at death, the soul turns into a dove.
2. In Visigoth and Romanesque art, it represents souls.
3. In Hinduism, the dove represents the spirit. (Perhaps this is where David's confusion lies, except of course that his term "Spirit of God" wouldn't apply, and the context of the KJV title page engraving is hardly representative of Hinduism!)
4. The dove was sacred to Zeus, to Athena as a symbol of the renewal of life, and to Aphrodite as a symbol of love.
5. To the ancient Egyptians, it signified innocence.
6. In Islam the dove is the protector of Mohammed.
7. In China, the dove represents longevity and orderliness.
8. In Japan, the dove is associated with the war god Hachiman.
9. In Jewish history, the dove was sometimes sacrificed for a mother's purification after childbirth.
10. The dove is sometimes an emblem of Israel.
11. In Christianity, the dove often symbolizes the Holy Spirit, in addition to the "heavenly messenger". In Genesis 8:8-10, the dove was the first sign given of restoration after the great flood, and its connection to peace was forever established by bringing the olive branch to the Ark. In Psalm 55:6, the wings of the dove are associated with rest.

As we can see, there is no such thing as "the pagan symbol" in the first instance because "pagan" is a generic word referring to a multiplicity of cultures which do not worship God.

In the second instance, in each of these pagan cultures the dove symbology had its own unique meaning to that culture.

Why, one is led to wonder, does David Bay ignore the obvious and instead state the indefensible? Does he think his readership is that gullible and misinformed?

***This information was gleaned from Cemetery Symbols Found in Forest Lawn Cemetery, Buffalo, NY. See http://ah.bfn.org/a/forestL/symbols/

Part 5 – A Response to David Bay's claim

Wherefore putting away lying, speak every man truth with his neighbour: for we are members with one another. Neither give place to the devil. Let no corrupt communication proceed out of your mouth, but that which is good to the use of edifying, that it may minister grace unto the hearers. (Ephesians 4: 25,27,29 KJV)

Part 6 – A Response to David Bay's four claims

about the 1611 KJV title page being composed of "occult, Rosicrucian, Kabbalistic symbols placed there by Francis Bacon and his Knights of the Helmet", summarized from Article 1001 as follows:

From page 5-6: "The lower hem of the garment worn by the High Priest has symbols filling up this space (that) are Luciferic All-Seeing Eyes".

From page 6-7: The lower middle image depicts a "swan with young brood pecking her breast", part of the "five steps to immortality according to Rosicrucianism".

From page 8-9: The lower right image depicts a "Satanic Phoenix Bird...holding an ink well up to the Perfected Man... in the Lower World".

From page 9-11: The upper centre area depicts a "man (in the Celestial/Middle World) with the X", X being "the sign of Osiris, the great Egyptian sun god; "the Chaldean sky god; the ancient solar god", etc.

Before responding to these claims, it may be of interest to the reader to realize the motive behind these attacks against the King James Version. This motive is provided verbatim from a January 14, 2006 e-mail from Ron Riffe to a Cutting Edge subscriber. Ron Riffe was defrocked as "pastor" of Cutting Edge Ministries on April 27, 2006 likely for "spilling the beans" and for insubordination to his "superior", David Bay.

Following are his words:

"Our intent is to put an end to such harsh and un-Christlike responses from the 'King James-only' crowd by **proving beyond a reasonable doubt** that the 1611 King James Version was edited by the Rosicrucian/Freemason Francis Bacon and his band of intellectuals known as the 'Order of the Helmet'". (Emphasis mine)

After reviewing the section from **Part 5** of this rebuttal entitled **"Proving one's allegations in a court of law"**, it appears that Cutting Edge sees this as a criminal matter. So be it.

1611 KJV title page

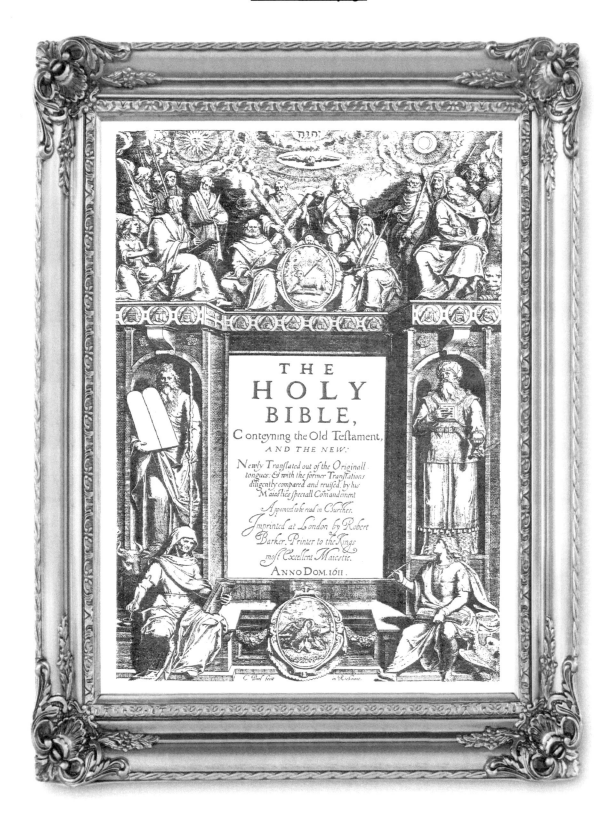

Part 6 – A Response to David Bay's four claims

The meaning of the symbolism associated with the High Priest

Of all the images put forward in David Bay's attack on the KJV – the engraved copperplate title page depictions, the genealogy pages, the woodcut headpiece and the woodcut letters – the high priest symbolism was the most difficult to "get a handle on". After scouring dozens of books, website articles, dictionaries and encyclopedias, there was no comprehensive explanation for the symbolism associated with the high priest (as depicted on the 1611 KJV frontispiece) to be found. I finally realized that I had done a great disservice to the very book I was claiming to defend…perhaps the meaning was contained therein!

There are many excellent websites, in addition to Exodus Chapter 28 and 39, that describe the vestments of the high priest. If the reader is not familiar with these facts, I highly recommend that they become so in order to appreciate the significance of the following information. Why?

The scripture verses to be cited as proof texts offer a meaning which is a departure from that of every reference work, secular and religious, on who this high priest is and 'why all the eyes'?

The key, then, to understanding the meaning is identifying this high priest, who is NOT Aaron. This misidentification is understandable, due to the close association of Moses (shown on the left of the frontispiece with the tablets on which the ten commandments were engraved) and Aaron in the Old Testament. This image of the high priest also serves to illustrate the problem we can run into when we either don't understand the definition of a symbol and an emblem, or else confuse the two.

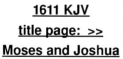

**1611 KJV title page: >>
Moses and Joshua**

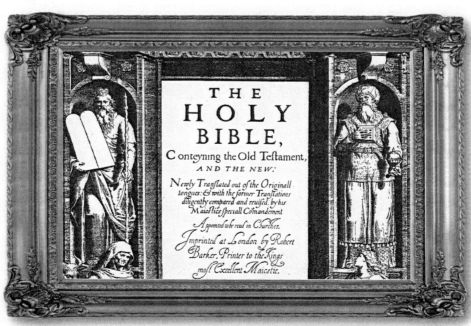

This image is, in fact, an <u>emblem</u> that can be taken at face value when seen as the engraver Cornelis Boel saw as he engraved it, when he had the scriptures opened to Zechariah Chapter 3 and 4 for this part of his master work. Open your King James Version to these chapters and compare these verses with this emblem.

<u><< 1611 KJV title page:</u>
<u>Joshua, the high priest</u>

Zech. 3:1 – And he shewed me Joshua the high priest standing before the angel of the Lord, and Satan standing at his right hand to resist him.

On the frontispiece, **<u>Joshua</u> the high priest** is **standing before the angel of the Lord** (shown kneeling beside Matthew "the evangelist" in the upper left hand corner), and **Satan** is **standing at his right hand to resist him** (to the upper right of Joshua, in the shadows over the picture of the paschal lamb, with a sickle in his hand).

Zech. 3:5 – And I said, Let them set a fair mitre upon his head. So they set a fair mitre upon his head, and clothed him with garments. And the angel of the Lord stood by.

Joshua is standing, **clothed with** the **garments** of the high priest, as described in Exodus Chapter 28 and 39. **A fair mitre** (turban), signifying righteousness and authority, has been **set upon his head. And the angel of the Lord** is **standing by** (in front and to one side of Satan, and next to the "man with the X" (who we'll be getting to in due time). The reason I say that this is an angel, and not one of the twelve disciples, is that he is holding an inkwell and has an appearance similar to the angel kneeling next to Matthew. Symbolically, another disciple would not be performing this function. There is also good reason to believe that this angel is none other than the archangel Michael, who is standing between Joshua and Satan, thus "hindering" Satan symbolically.

Zech. 3:8 – Here now, O Joshua the high priest, thou, and thy fellows that sit before thee: for they are men wondered at: for, behold, I will bring forth my servant the BRANCH.

Joshua the high priest is standing in behind **thy fellows** (the four evangelists – Matthew and Mark – in the corners above and before him…and Luke and John – in the corners below and before him) **that sit before thee. They are men wondered at** because they are prefigured here (in the sense of being at the time of Joshua), and will be **brought forth** (in the sense of being called) by **my servant the BRANCH** (the pre-incarnate Christ).

We'll now deal with the matter of the eyes on the lower part of the full-length undergarment (the "coat" – see Exodus 28:39).

Zech. 3:9 – For behold, the stone that I have laid before Joshua; upon one stone shall be seven eyes: behold, I will engrave the engraving thereof, saith the Lord of hosts, and I will remove the iniquity of that land in one day.

Zech. 4:10b – they are the eyes of the Lord, which run to and fro through the whole earth.

Joshua is now a type for Christ, **the stone** God the Father **laid before Joshua** (before Abraham was I AM) which the builders would refuse (Ps. 118:22 et al). **Upon this one stone shall be seven eyes** (Rev. 4:5 and 5:6).

Jesus Christ, the **Lord of hosts** and Righteous High Priest, is now promising the children of Israel: **I will engrave the engraving thereof** not with ink or in tables of stone, but in fleshy tables of the heart (II Cor. 3:3 and 3:7-18) when he comes to **remove the iniquity of that land in one day** (Zech. Chapter 14 et al).

Joshua, in this depiction as high priest, is prefiguring two attributes of the deity of Jesus Christ from Zech. 4:10: the **eyes of the Lord** are in everyplace (on the robe) Prov.15:3 - omniscience, and **which run to and fro through the whole earth** (as depicted by the globe in his left hand) II Chron.16:9a - omnipresence.

1611 KJV title page:
depiction of eyes on Joshua's coat

43

Part 6 – A Response to David Bay's four claims

1611 KJV title page: depiction of "Globe"

There is much more that could be said about the other vestments of the high priest – the breastplate, the ephod, etc., but since this discussion wouldn't bear directly in responding to the bizarre claims of David Bay, we'll leave it at that.

As far as Bay's claim that the eyes on the garment are depictions of "Luciferic All-Seeing Eyes", this is just more deception and misinformation, something that he is proficient at. For example, the Udjat Eye of Horus with the two appendages under the eye is totally different from the eyes on the bottom of the high priest's robe. It seems that David has spent too much time in the Egyptian Meditation Room under the tutelage of Dr. Bob Hieronimus, the self-proclaimed Artist of Savitria and author of the book that is the inspiration for David's DVDs on the *Secret Mysteries of America's Beginnings*. Dr. Bob's book has certainly received rave reviews by like-minded New Agers and Rosicrucians such as Whitley Strieber, Shirley Maclaine and David A. Burnett (Grand Councillor Emeritus of the AMORC).

The other attempt to deceive his readers by quoting "Rosicrucian author" Frances Yates (doubly misspelled as previously noted), is a misguided inference that any commonly-used "symbol" in the culture that is common to any "occult" group (such as a depiction of an eye) is inherently evil and therefore one of "Satan's devices". This is patently ridiculous! I suppose that means we have to hang the label "occult, Luciferian, Rosicrucian, Masonic and Kabbalistic" onto the countless organizations that have adopted a variation of the eye as their logo!

I'll leave it to the "jury" to decide who the "blind modern-day Christians" are. Of course, they couldn't possibly be the ones who would favourably quote blind modern-day Rosicrucian and Masonic leaders!

Part 6 – A Response to David Bay's four claims

The meaning of the "the swan with young brood pecking her breast"

With this emblem, we continue to build our case that the 1611 King James Version title page, rather than being assembled by nefarious Rosicrucian Kabbalists and occultists as David Bay and his fellow charlatans say, was drawn and engraved by Cornelis Boel, and is in fact a beautiful copperplate which perfectly portrays the content of the text.

Thus far, we have seen the appropriateness of the tetragrammaton and dove, the symmetry of Moses and Joshua in their roles as lawgiver and high priest, as well as the perfect harmony between the depiction of Joshua the high priest in Zechariah 3 and 4 with the vestments and positioning of Joshua, the four evangelists, the angels and Satan on this magnificent frontispiece.

It's sad but predictable that David Bay goes back yet again to his Rosicrucian magus for wisdom with respect to the meaning of the "swan with young brood" emblem. A young Manley Hall "tells" David what he has learned from his spare-time readings of esoteric literature at the New York Public Library while employed as a bank clerk, and then writes a book called *The Secret Teachings of All Ages* (not All "The" Ages, as David says). This book seems to be treated like eye salve by David.

As with Bay's writings, Hall's are an admixture of fact, fiction, half-truths, speculation and error…which Bay buys into with great enthusiasm. For instance, Bay claims that this "Mother Bird with her young" is

Mythological Phoenix – typical depiction over flames (no young brood)

"one of the most popular Rosicrucian scenes of all time" but doesn't tell us his source. From David Letterman's "Top Ten" list perhaps? He also claims that the "phoenix, pelican and swan…are used interchangeably in these scenes". This may be true for Rosicrucianism but it's not true in sixteenth and early seventeenth century emblemata, which is prior to the existence of any published Rosicrucian writings, particularly with respect to the matter of illustrations. The practise among the Rosicrucians and Freemasons of "hijacking hieroglyphics", such as the pelican in her piety with a superimposed compass and rose-covered cross, didn't come until later when artists such as Eliphas Levi arrived on the scene. The birds used interchangeably in this emblem are the pelican and swan…the phoenix is used by itself, usually over enflamed wood and ashes.

Part 6 - A Response to David Bay's four claims

See:

1. Epiphanius' *Physiologus*, printed in 1588 by Christopher Plantin...concerning the pelican (and her young).

2. McKerrow's *Printers' & Publishers Devices in England & Scotland*: 1485-1640 Device No. 123, 125a and 125b of a pelican in her piety, with the monogram of Richard Jugge. Used in various books, including Bibles, from 1552-1595.

3. Whitney's *A Choice of Emblemes,* printed in 1586, page 87, showing a picture of a pelican with her young.

4. Wither's *A Collection of Emblemes*, printed in 1635, page 24, with the caption "Our pelican, by bleeding thus, Fulfill'd the Law, and cured Us".

Cornelis Boel's cartouche of the pelican in her piety on the KJV title page is in keeping with the above-noted sample emblems, which came with mottos, poems or epigrams to explain the meaning and significance of the illustration to the reader.

1611 KJV title page: Pelican in her piety

Part 6 – A Response to David Bay's four claims

Consider the poem to go with the caption on Wither's depiction of the pelican with her young:

> Looke here, and marke (her fickly birds to feed)
> How freely this kinde *Pelican* doth bleed.
> See how (when other Salves could not be found)
> To cure their sorrowes, she, herself doth wound;
> And, when this holy *Emblem*, thou shalt see,
> Lift up thy soule to him, who dy'd for thee.
> For, this our Hieroglyphick would exresse
> That *Pelican*, which in the *Wildernesse*
> Of this vast *World*, was left (as all alone)
> Our miserable *Nature* to bemone;
> And, in whose eyes, the teares of pitty stood,
> When he beheld his owne unthankfull *Brood*
> His *Favours*, and his *Mercies*, then, contemne,
> When with his wings he would have brooded them.

Bay's sordid attempt to tar this beautiful cartouche of the pelican and her young, as depicted on the KJV title page, with the blackness of Rosicrucianism and Freemasonry is unconscionable.

The lower right image (supposedly) depicts a Satanic Phoenix Bird

We now come to David's next accusation, namely that "there is no doubt whatsoever that this (image in the lower right of the title page) is (the) Satanic Phoenix Bird".

This statement is one of many that show how profoundly ignorant David Bay is with respect to even a rudimentary understanding of this title page, and seemingly of the whole matter of emblems and symbols. This is also another example of "saying so doesn't make it so".

Who told David that this is a phoenix bird? A little birdie perhaps? No, we find out that David has been listening to Manley Hall again, as well as his "expert witness", "former witch" Bill Schnoebelen. We don't even need to listen to more occult lore, this time about the phoenix, from David and his friends. Why? Because this is an **emblem**, not a symbol and it is an **eagle**, not a phoenix.

How do we know this when David says "there is no doubt whatsoever that this is a Satanic Phoenix Bird"? Very simple. **This frontispiece depicts the four evangelists alongside their traditional emblems.** References to the four disciples (evangelists) and their emblems date back to the writings of Bishop Iranaeus in the 2nd century A.D. Below are examples.

Part 6 - A Response to David Bay's four claims

But first, here is the standard arrangement, as depicted on the 1611 KJV title page:

Matthew and his emblem, an angel

Mark and his emblem, a lion

Luke and his emblem, an ox (or bull)

John and his emblem, an eagle

Part 6 – A Response to David Bay's four claims

For proof of these symbols being traditionally associated with the four evangelists, one can simply click onto http://en.wikipedia.org/wiki/Four_Evangelists.

For proof of the extensive use of this evangelist/symbol arrangement over the last one thousand, nine hundred years, one can simply click onto http://catholic-resources.org/Art/Evangelists_Symbols.htm.

Of particular interest to the King James Bible believer is that this evangelist/emblem tradition pre-dates Roman Catholicism, due to its reference in the writings of Iranaeus. Contrary to the claims of Catholicism, their "founding father" was not the apostle Peter, but Augustine, who lived from 354 - 430 A.D., some two and a half centuries after Iranaeus. It is to be expected that Roman Catholicism, due to its heavy dependence on iconography, would embrace the idea of emblems for the four evangelists, and thus we find this parallel lineage in Protestant and Catholic artwork.

We'll next look at what Rosemary Freeman, former lecturer at Birkbeck College in England had to say regarding the context of the use of this evangelist/emblem imagery in the English emblem tradition of the 16th and 17th centuries. In writing the foreword to Freeman's book entitled *English Emblem Books* published in 1948, E.M.W. Tillyard states that "Miss Freeman has mastered her subject, and, as well as presenting a scholarly survey of the whole field, has given us an insight into the general psychology of the time which is of great interest to students of history and literature alike".

On page 90-91, Miss Freeman states that "An interest in the emblematic had long been present in decoration; indeed, as was pointed out in Chapter 2, **in England** the essential features of the emblem book appear there before they are found in literary form, and **certain subjects akin to, or even identical with, the themes in emblem books occur frequently among the devices used.** The Nine Worthies, the Four Seasons, the Four Elements, **The Four Evangelists**, the Five Senses, the Three Theological Virtues-all **had to make their appearance sooner or later on the ceilings and panels of houses just as they had appeared in other forms in the past.**"

Following, then, are examples of wood blocks or copperplate engravings where the four evangelists with their emblems are shown in their standard arrangement as depicted on the title page of the 1611 King James Version:
1. Woodcut impression of *The Virgin and Child in a Glory, with the Signs of the Evangelists,* printed in 1129, Paris. On display in the Historisches Museum, Basle.
2. Wood block device (103 x 73 mm.) used by the printer William Bretton, Paris, in various publications from 1505 to 1522.
3. Title page of Tyndale's *Translation of the New Testament,* Printed in 1536.
4. Title page of Bishops' Bible, printed by Robert Barker in 1602.

Things don't get any better for David Bay as we move on to his next allegation.

Part 6 – A Response to David Bay's four claims

The meaning of "the man with the X"

According to David Bay in Article 1001, his "journey (to prove that the 1611 King James Version was a product of Rosicrucian Kabbalists) began in June 1997". Judging by his efforts so far he should have

stayed in the Toys, Trains, Games and Puzzles arena. The only thing we can perhaps be thankful for, is that, based on the nine year incubation period for this "egg", we will be spared another "aerial bomb" for another nine years. Rather than at the outset recognizing that this image is an emblem, David launches into a series of bombastic gyrations that would do a stunt pilot proud. Texe Marrs, in his latest book *Codex Magica: The Innermost Secrets of the Illuminati Beckon You!*, is now misrepresented to "prove" that Bay's parallel world exists on the title page of the 1611 King James Version. Such is not the case.

1611 KJV title page: "the man with the X"

Much like the Bishops' Bible was used by the KJV translators (in keeping with the King's instructions) as a basis (or starting point) for the new text, the frontispiece from the Bishops' Bible was used by Cornelis Boel as a template for the KJV frontispiece. By implication, this meant that Boel had the authority, within limits, to make certain changes…changes which are obvious in the format and graphics, but less obvious in the details…details that are important.

1611 KJV title page: Jude, Thomas, Matthias, Bartholomew

We have, so far, identified the two Old Testament representatives on the title page, those being Moses and Joshua. We have also established the identity of the "four evangelists" (Matthew, Mark, Luke and John, with their traditional emblems), the two angels (one kneeling and one standing) and Satan.

Four apostles are standing, clustered behind Matthew, and they are from left to right, Jude (with his emblem the sword), Thomas (with spear), Matthias (with halberd) and Bartholomew (with knife).

Part 6 – A Response to David Bay's four claims

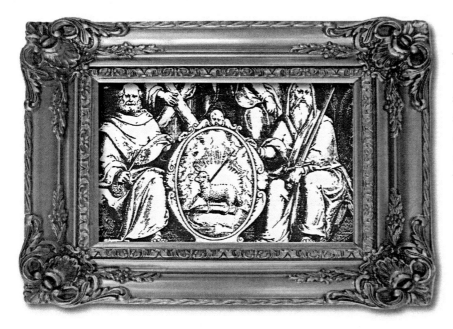

Two more apostles, Peter (with keys) and Paul (with sword), are seated on each side of the Paschal Lamb cartouche. Paul is not shown on the Bishops' Bible frontispiece, but this position on the KJV frontispiece coupled with his emblem requires this to be him.

<< 1611 KJV title page:
Peter and Paul

We have another cluster of four men standing behind the evangelist Mark. The two to our left are the apostles Simon Zelotes (with hacksaw) and James the Less (with long club).

1611 KJV title page: >>
Simon Zelotes and James the Less
(Mark on far right)

<< 1611 KJV title page: James the Greater and Philip (Mark on lower left)

It remains that the two to the right of Mark must then be James the Greater (with staff) and Philip (with spear), except for one thing. James is shown with a pilgrim's (wide-brimmed) hat on the Bishops' Bible while the KJV frontispiece shows him with the hat, hairstyle and facial features of Erasmus. This figure, then, must have the dual identity of James the Greater and Erasmus. Let's now identify the apostle with the cross.

This image is none other than "*St. Andrew Carrying the Cross*", and is an almost exact replica of a drawing by Hans Holbein the Younger, and bearing that title. This pen and black ink drawing was done in 1527.

Holbein drawing >>

Part 6 – A Response to David Bay's four claims

Further confirmation is found on **page 54 of The Heroicall Devices of M. Claudius Paradin**, London edition, 1591. This epigram follows:

Two Lawrell boughs rubbed hard together (if we shall credite what Pliny hath recorded) yeeld fire forth by long and continuall chastening. Manie are of opinion also, that the bones of a Lion do the same. So likewise most certaine it is, that no little danger falleth us, when mightie men meet together, that the old proverbe may be verified which faith, *Dura duris non quadrare*, in ploughing or tilling of the ground, hard things agree not together. The description of this symbole or figure appertaineth to the crosse of saint Andrew..."

It is important to keep in mind that Hans Holbein the Younger, a prolific Flemish painter of the first rank, worked in England for many years doing paintings for the royal family and other families connected with the court of Henry VIII (1526-28, 1532-43). During the rest of his career he resided in Basel (1515-1526, 1528, 1531-32).

It is apparent, by the amazing likeness of Cornelis Boel's engraving of St. Andrew carrying the cross (on the 1611 KJV title page) to Holbein's drawing (dated 1527), that Boel, a Flemish artist and engraver also working in England was well aware of Holbein's body of work. It was this awareness and admiration that led him, I believe, to use Holbein's drawing of Andrew as a template for his later work. Holbein, while in Basel, did a number of portraitures of none other than Desiderius Erasmus. If one compares these portraitures, noting especially the narrow face and distinctive hat, the identification of Erasmus on the KJV title page is readily made. The other reason I believe that this figure behind the evangelist Mark is both James and Erasmus (keeping in mind that all the apostles are accounted for) is that Erasmus' Greek New Testament (amongst whose writers he is standing) almost single-handedly opened the floodgates of Renaissance scholarship onto numerous vernacular translations of the glorious gospel of Jesus Christ.

Part 6 - A Response to David Bay's four claims

It is interesting that Philip, an apostle to the Gentiles, is **speaking** to Erasmus / James. To the King James Bible believer, this represents the transmission of the inspired, preserved words of God.

Since David Bay doesn't seem to be any help with things pertaining to the real world, and especially pertaining to emblems and symbols, let's finish our examination of the 1611 KJV title page with a final comment with respect to **why the apostle holding the keys has to be Peter**. Take a look at Matthew 16:16-19, and with these verses I close this part of the rebuttal.

> 16 And Simon Peter answered and said, Thou art the Christ, the Son of the Living God.
>
> 17 And Jesus answered and said unto him, Blessed art thou, Simon Barjona: for flesh and blood hath not revealed it unto thee, but my Father which is in heaven.
>
> 18 And I say also unto thee, **That thou art Peter**, and upon this rock I will build my church; and the gates of hell shall not prevail against it.
>
> 19 And **I will give unto thee the keys of the kingdom of heaven**: and whatsoever thou shalt bind on earth shall be bound in heaven: and whatsoever thou shalt loose on earth shall be loosed in heaven.

Dear reader, are you going to "take your place" alongside the saints so perfectly depicted on this masterpiece of engraving. If so, you also have access to these keys, with the concomitant ability to bind those who attack the church, the Living Word and the written word.

David Bay is claiming, in effect, that this frontispiece is a scene from hell. Is that what you believe?

If not, you also have the ability to "**loose on earth**" (**See 1 Tim. 4:1,2**), to pray that the truth will set people bound in the throes of Rosicrucianism, Freemasonry and the doctrines of devils free.

Truth comes in many guises. Don't be fooled by wolves in sheep's clothing.

Part 7 – A Response to David Bay's claim

that the "upper portion of 'page lii' in the 1611 KJV Bible" contains "dozens and dozens of Masonic Handshakes, proving once again our contention that Sir Francis Bacon – the consummate Kabbalist Master of his day – had his hands on the Bible".
From Article 1001 and 1002.

The only conclusion I can come to after listening to this whopper is that David is now delirious and delusional. Is there a doctor in the house? Perhaps David has succumbed to a curse from the Udjat Eye of Horus in Dr. Bob's Egyptian Meditation Room (see part 6, page 3).

No person in their right mind, surely, could see these hands for anything else than what is OBVIOUSLY STATED IN THE SCRIPTURE VERSES THAT ARE UNDER THE NAME OF THE PERSON ASSOCIATED WITH EACH HAND.

THESE ARE NOT HANDSHAKES BUT HANDS JOINED IN HOLY MATRIMONY.

1611 KJV: section from genealogy pages

Think about this. The representation of these clasped hands, with their meaning stated in EVERY case as being a husband and wife relationship (many of the males having multiple wives), is there for even the neophyte to see. What other options are there, other than delirium and delusion, when David spends **THE LAST PART OF HIS ARTICLE 1001 AND ALL OF ARTICLE 1002** under the delusion that these are "Masonic Handshakes"?

Part 7 – A Response to David Bay's claim

If David cannot even grasp this simple concept of a husband and wife holding hands, and this fact gets out to his Baconian handlers, I can see David getting a hand signal, as in "good-bye".

I haven't reached this conclusion about David Bay's state of mind hastily, or without considering the evidence. Consider the following facts that we have brought to light:

1) David titles his articles attacking the King James Version as "Defending the King James Version". (A double minded man is unstable in all his ways.)

2) David Bay primarily relies on Rosicrucians, Freemasons, Baconians and occultists to "Defend the King James Version". This is akin to hiring a player from the opposing soccer team to defend your goal.

3) Many of David's attacks centre on the fallacy of "occult symbols" in the KJV. David has demonstrated that he doesn't know the difference between an emblem and a symbol, and has demonstrated a profound absence of knowledge in the whole area of frontispieces, woodcuts and ornamental devices as they were used in the sixteenth and seventeenth centuries. This is obvious by the dearth of citations.

4) David has based his attack on the underlying fallacy of a conspiracy among a phantom secret society, the Knights of the Helmet. There is a complete absence of documentation on the existence of this "secret society" except as a playful satire on one evening at Gray's Inn. Francis Bacon has likewise been shown to be a phantom as far as having any proven influence on any aspects of the production of the 1611 or 1619 King James Version.

5) David's analysis of the 1611 KJV title page has been demonstrated to be the vain babblings of a troubled mind. How else could one describe such a bizarre claim…a claim that, in effect, portrays this "comely frontispiece" (from a scholarly work by that name) as a scene from hell. This claim is astonishing, mind-boggling and without any basis in the real world…only in a parallel (delusional) world.

Part 8 – A Response to David Bay's claim

that Pan "the Greek god of sexual lust and orgies is depicted prominently twice in the original 1611 KJV Bible". From Article 1003.

In positing this latest claim, David Bay has decided to break away from his Rosicrucian and Baconian handlers, enter the nearest available phone booth, and assume the persona of pseudo-Icarus in soaring to new heights of folly. Much like the large-eyed rove beetle which is able to propel itself on the surface of the water (and presumably attract a mate) by glandular emissions, David is endeavouring to function on the surface (of the ideas of others) and attract the attention of the casual voyeur by disseminating his vision of giant phalli in the KJV Bible. This is truly a pathetic sight because, as is indicated above, none of his Rosicrucian/Baconian mentors have even had the temerity to go on record with this type of "vision".

HEARE, ICARVS with mountinge vp alofte,
Came headlonge downe, and fell into the Sea:
His waxed winges, the sonne did make so softe,
They melted straighte, and feathers fell awaie:
    So, whilste he flewe, and of no dowbte did care,
    He mooüde his armes, but loe, the same were bare.

Part 8 – A Response to David Bay's claim

Let's look at two examples which are typical of Rosicrucian/Baconian authors in describing this headpiece, which is usually referred to as either a Pan Headpiece or Archer Device.

Firstly, from www.prs.org/gallery-bacon.htm we read in the article titled **Francis Bacon's Ciphers**, under *A Cryptic Headpiece from Raleigh's History of the World*:

> Many documents influenced by Baconian philosophy – or intended to conceal Baconian or Rosicrucian cryptograms – use certain conventional designs at the beginning and end of chapters, which reveal to the initiated the presence of concealed information. The above ornamental scroll has long been accepted as proof of the presence of Baconian influence and is to be found only in a certain number of rare volumes, all of which contain Baconian cryptograms. These cipher messages were placed in the books either by Bacon himself or by contemporary and subsequent authors belonging to the same secret society which Bacon served with his remarkable knowledge of ciphers and enigmas. Variants of this headpiece adorn the *Great Shakespearean Folio* (1623); Bacon's *Novum Organum* (1620); the *St. James Bible* (1611); Spenser's *Faerie Queene* (1611); and Sir Walter Raleigh's *History of the World* (1614).

Secondly, from www.sirbacon.org we read in ***Francis Bacon and the Secret of Ornamental Devices*** by Mather Walker (August, 2002), under **The Archer Device**:

> The meaning of the Archer device is fairly obvious also. For Bacon, Pan represented universal nature, and to the acquisition of all knowledge as "the Hunt of Pan"…Therefore, the central figure in the emblem is Pan, shown by the fact that He was god of hunters, by the shaggy nature of his legs, and by the fivefold headdress…in the emblem the hounds of the chase are depicted as turned toward Pan, the central figure, with their noses to the ground, ie. hot on the scent of Pan, or the search for knowledge. The archers are also turned toward the central figure of Pan, but their arrows are dipped low so they are actually directed about half way between Pan and the clusters of grapes beneath him…Here also are seen the rabbits, emblem of…vigilance… and here are seen the running vines of ivy…continually growing. The blossoms are shown with two directed straight up, and two directed outward to the reader, since Bacon said one beam of knowledge is directed upward toward God, and one toward man. The two peacocks held by the seated figure tells us by (sic) the "Archer" device was used to mark the more prestigious works.

Part 8 – A Response to David Bay's claim

David Bay, as is obvious in the first paragraph of his Article 1003, is engorged with the delusion of success with respect to his vision of "Masonic Handshakes" in Article 1002. Freed from the fetters of reality and decorum, David can now revel in treating his readers to tales of lechery, lust and debauchery…all in the name of "Defending the King James Version", of course.

Unfortunately for David, though, while he is waxing eloquent in orgiastic tales of Wicca and Greek mythology, he fails to notice that the wax on his new wings is starting to melt.

As has been stated in previous parts of this rebuttal, there is a decided difference between emblems and symbols…an understanding of which is crucial when dealing with a subject matter of this importance. The difficulty with this headpiece, which is in part inferred by the two titles attributed by Rosicrucian/Baconian writers, is that it can be taken to be an emblem or a symbol, or perhaps even both. While it is seemingly apparent that the figure at the centre of this headpiece is Pan (although some might say a combination of Pan and Bacchus), there is at least one meaning for this ornamental device that disagrees with the Rosicrucian/Baconian view.

Furthermore, despite the claims of Rosicrucian, Baconian and Masonic scholars, this headpiece is known as a printer's or publisher's device, not an author's or writer's device, for good reason. These devices, as was mentioned earlier in this rebuttal, were the property of printers and publishers, and were traded, passed down or shared with other printers and publishers throughout Europe during this period. Most, but not all, of these devices used in England and Scotland between 1485 and 1640 are depicted, with their genealogies, in a book by that name written by Ronald B. McKerrow, and published in London in 1913. Perhaps David Bay, in misquoting his Rosicrucian friends by calling this the "Hunt For Pan" headpiece instead of the "Hunt of Pan" headpiece has stumbled, albeit unwittingly, onto something which has seemingly confounded everyone to date…that being, Where did this printer's or publisher's device come from? McKerrow does not show this device in his book, although he has co-written a later book ***Title-Page Borders used in England and Scotland, 1485-1640*** which may provide a clue (this headpiece was used on some title pages). This book has been ordered from a bookseller in New York, and has been delayed in shipping due to flooding in their area. Due to the likelihood that this device did not originate in England or Scotland, I have also endeavoured to trace the provenance of this headpiece by identifying where it was first used in England, and then determining where it came from on the European mainland. We'll update progress on this "hunt for the Pan headpiece" in an appendix.

Returning to the matter of this printer's or publisher's device being an emblem or a symbol, or both, it is this writer's conclusion that, based on the one interpretation already given above by Mather Walker, and one about to be given by this writer, that this has to be a symbol. Remember that a symbol can be, and often is, infused with a multiplicity of meanings. It is essential, therefore, to examine the symbol in its context, the context in this case being its use in two places of the 1611 King James Version of the Bible, to determine what the likeliest meaning is.

Part 8 – A Response to David Bay's claim

Before we do that, due to the contortions that David Bay and his Rosicrucian/Baconian mentors go through to "prove" Baconian authorship of Spenser's works, Shakespeare's works and Raleigh's works, amongst others, we'll bring some more background information to light in order to properly evaluate the claims of David Bay, and of those he is in many cases parroting.

As noted in the passage from *A Cryptic Headpiece* above, Rosicrucians (and those, like Bay, who take them at their word) boldly declare Bacon's impress on various published works – works published before Bacon's writing career began, during his writing years and after his death. The rationale for this can be summed up in a motto on www.sirbacon.org/abvol12.htm, which says "One stem – many branches". In attempting to attribute Baconian authorship or major influence on dozens, if not hundreds, of books, Rosicrucians and Baconians confer god-like status on Bacon. Consider these words from Mather Walker in ***Francis Bacon and the Secret of Ornamental Devices*** from the section under **The Archer Device**, quoted above:

> I end this series of articles as I began – amazed at that fantastic being Francis Bacon. The scope of his accomplishments was absolutely astounding. During the romantic period when Shakespeare was deified, one of his admirers waxed hyperbolic, raving, "Next to God Shakespeare created most". If he had known the full extent of Bacon's creativity he might have been tempted to say, "Next to Bacon God created most."

This "Archer" device or Pan Headpiece, as stated by Walker, "was used to mark the more prestigious works" (of Francis Bacon and his secret society). Thus the claim of Baconian authorship, editorship, etc. on works such as Spenser's *Faerie Queene* (1611), the *King James Bible* (1611), Raleigh's *History of the World* (1614) and the *Great Shakespeare Folio* (1623), along with Bacon's own *Novum Organum* (1620)… one stem (the creator-god Bacon) and many branches (the great works of the day as noted above, plus those of Marlowe, Ben Jonson - the list goes on and on).

What the Rosicrucian and Baconian apologists don't mention (or aren't aware of) are the books with this device that don't support their assertions. Two examples are:

1. *Descrittione del Regno di Scotia, et delle isole sue adiacenti,* a free translation of Hector Boece's *Hystory and Croniklis of Scotland* by Petruccio Ubaldini, under the (fictitious) imprint of John Wolfe, printed in London in 1588.

   (Bacon was hardly in a position to effect any influence on an Italian translation of a book about the History of Scotland, having just been elevated, after a nine year residency, as a Reader of Gray's Inn along with his duties as a fledgling parliamentarian.)

2. *English New Testament Rheims-Bishops' Parallel Version of the Bible.* 1601.Second printing. Printed by G.B.(George Bishop) for W. Fulke. London.

(As with the above example, there is no evidence to indicate any rhyme or reason for Bacon's involvement in a work such as this. This parallel Bible was completely foreign to what he was occupying his time with, namely matters of the Privy Council in the court of Queen Elizabeth. See *Hostage to Fortune: The Troubled Life of Francis Bacon* – pp. 209-262.)

We'll next show just how much at odds so-called Rosicrucian/Baconian scholarship can be with the documented type of scholarship recognized in the academic world at large.

In order to do this, let's see what the two interpretations of the title page imagery from **Walter Ralegh's** ***History of the World*** *(shown below)*, first edition published anonymously in 1614, are. Following is the Rosicrucian/Baconian interpretation as stated in www.sirbacon.org/raleighall.html:

What was the mysterious knowledge which Sir Walter Ralegh possessed and which was declared to be detrimental to the British government?...Was Sir Walter Ralegh an important factor in the Bacon-Shakespere-Rosicrucian-Masonic enigma? Sir Walter Ralegh – soldier, courtier, statesman, writer, poet, philosopher, and explorer – was a scintillating figure at the court of Queen Elizabeth... The title page reproduced above was used by Ralegh's political foes as a powerful weapon against him. They convinced James I that the face of the central figure upholding the globe was a caricature of his own, and the enraged king ordered every copy of the engraving destroyed. But a few copies escaped the royal wrath: consequently the plate is extremely rare. The engraving is a mass of Rosicrucian and Masonic symbols, and the figures on the columns in all probability conceal a cryptogram. More significant still is the fact that on the page facing this plate is a headpiece (the "Archer" device) identical with that used in the 1623 Folio of "Shakespeare" and also in Bacon's *Novum Organum*.

The scholarly interpretation is admirably represented on pp.129-135 of Margery Corbett and Ronald Lightbown's ***The Comely Frontispiece: The Emblematic Title-Page in England***. We can only give brief excerpts from their superb analysis and interpretation, which when read in its entirety, makes the above quotation laughable in comparison.

Part 8 – A Response to David Bay's claim

The central figure, *Magistra vitae*, History herself, is in classical dress with gown, belted tunic and cloak; her head with a laurel wreath has a nimbus of rays of light; she upholds the globe which shows the known world; her feet press down on two figures reclining on the step, *Mors*, a skeleton, and a sleeping youth, *Oblivio*. The (decorated) columns are labelled on their bases, *Testis Temporv, Nvncia Vetvstatis, Lvx Veritatis, Vita Memoria* (and together with *Magistra vitae)* are the famous epithets from Cicero's *de Oratore*, II.xl.36...the side niches enclose the figure of *Experientia*...and *Veritas*...(which, together with *Magistra vitae*, form) the three allegorical figures, with adaptations in the case of the two last, from Philippe de Galle's *Prosopographia*, published in Antwerp between 1585 and the beginning of 1601. The two winged figures represent *Fama bona* (Good Fame) and *Fama mala* (Evil Fame). Above the globe is an enormous eye, *Providentia*.

Lest David Bay get engorged again with the vision of this "enormous eye" being the "All-Seeing Eye of Horus", **let's listen to what Sir Walter Ralegh (or Raleigh) himself has to say about the meaning of Providence as represented by this eye.** He devotes a section at the beginning of *History of the World* (book I, ch. I, pp.18f) to this very thing!

> God therefore, who is euery where present...whose eyes are upon the righteous, and his countenance against them that doe evil,...an infinite eye, beholding all things; and cannot therefore be esteemed as an idle looker on...God therefore who could onely be the cause of all, can only prouide for all, and sustaine all.

Corbett and Lightbown draw the following conclusion, based in part on various editions of the *Hieroglyphics of Horapollo* published in the 16th century, which also deal with this "great eye".

> By making the eye dominate the title-page Raleigh emphasises the biblical and Christian theme of God as the supreme moral judge, of his constant vigilance and his intervention in human affairs.

The reader is also reminded here of this writer's interpretation with regard to the identity of the high priest on the title page of the 1611 King James Version, along with the attributes of deity represented therein by the eyes and the globe.

We cannot leave this title page without mentioning one more fact, a fact which in itself demolishes any pretence of a valid interpretation from the Rosicrucian/Baconian camp. This fact, as stated by Margery Corbett and Ronald Lightbown, is as follows:

> (Ben) Jonson's *Minde of the Front.*, unsigned in the *History*, was included in *The Underwood* in the second volume of the Folio published in 1640 as *The Minde of the Frontispiece to a Booke*. The History was banned by James I some months after it appeared. The ban was probably lifted when Raleigh came out of prison in 1616 and there were several editions between 1617 and 1640. However, Jonson may have felt in the dangerous years before his death in 1637, that it was wiser not to avow his connection with it.

Part 8 – A Response to David Bay's claim

The meaning of the frontispiece for Raleigh's *History of the World* as given by Ben Jonson can be found at www.humanities-interactive.org/literature/bonfire/011d.html.

We'll now move on to an interpretation of the symbolism in the so-called Pan Headpiece or Archer device. We need to keep in mind that this is a printer's or publisher's device which was seemingly cut as a wood block in Belgium, France, Germany or Italy, and obtained by John Wolfe when he travelled abroad to these areas between 1569 and 1579 to study printing. According to http://special.lib.gla.ac.uk/exhibns/printing/wolfe.html Wolfe "was almost certainly working in Florence in 1576…and it is also probable that he lived in Frankfurt-am-Main for some time".

Wolfe started his career as a London printer in 1581 in partnership with Henry Kirkham, and went on his own in 1583. As far as I have been able to determine thus far, the first use of this device occurred, as noted above, in a book translated by Wolfe's Italian proof-reader, Petruccio Ubaldini, and falsely imprinted under Ubaldini's name in 1588 by John Wolfe. Did Ubaldini have something to do with the appearance of this device? More investigation is underway!

This device has elements which are similar to those found in ornamental devices used by Estienne (1550 Greek New Testament headpiece), Sambucus (*Emblemata*, Antwerp – 1564), and Giovio and Symeoni (*Del Capitano Girolamo* -1561 and 1562).

In offering this interpretation I also want to introduce some dynamics with respect to the introduction of this headpiece in English publications by John Wolfe. These are:

(1) this **Pan Headpiece** is found in the 1611 expanded edition of Edmund **Spenser's** *The Faerie Queene*, which also included the *Shepheardes Calender, and*

(2) the first edition of **Spenser's** *The Faerie Queen*, books i-iii, was printed in 1590 by **John Wolfe** for William Ponsonbie, and

(3) evidence for *The Faerie Queene* dates back to 1580 in a letter from Edmund Spenser to Gabriel Harvey requesting the return of the manuscript, and

(4) Ponsonbie was the publisher of all **Spenser's** works, except the *Shepheardes Calender* which was published in December 1579, and

(5) **John Wolfe** returned from Italy somewhere between 1577 and 1579, 1579 being the year in which Petruccio Ubaldini, a Florentine Protestant exile, was saved from imprisonment for debt by the intervention of the Privy Council, and

(6) **John Wolfe** hired Ubaldini a short time later, and Ubaldini served as Wolfe's proof-reader for a period of ten years, and

(7) **John Wolfe** first used the **Pan Headpiece** in a translation by Ubaldini in 1588.

Part 8 - A Response to David Bay's claim

Based on the above dynamics, I contend that it is much more plausible that this Pan Headpiece is associated with Edmund Spenser, not Francis Bacon. In fact, Francis Bacon can be completely eliminated from the equation due to the fact that he was a youth of 18 years of age in 1579, and had just returned from Paris, France and the custody of the foreign ambassador Sir Amias Paulet for his father's funeral. The year 1579 is significant due to the publication of Spenser's **The Shepheardes Calender**, his first major work, and which gives the answer for the more plausible meaning of the Pan Headpiece than that offered by the Rosicrucian/Baconian camp.

The Shepheardes Calender was published anonymously in 1579 by Hugh Singleton, "the radical Puritan propagandist", who just prior to its publication had narrowly escaped having his right hand cut off (his friends John Stubbs and William Page weren't so fortunate) for tirades against the proposed marriage of Queen Elizabeth to the French Catholic Alencon. The marriage did not come about, but the thinly veiled allegory was Spenser's warning, like that of Singleton and his friends, of the dangers to England inherent in the proposed marriage of Queen Elizabeth to the Catholic Frenchman. *The Shepheardes Calender* consists of twelve eclogues, and represents both the changes that take place over the twelve months of the year and the changes in the drama of the human experience. Each eclogue is formatted into name, woodcut, argument, eclogue, emblem and gloss...the gloss, or interpretation, in each case written by "E.K.", presumed to be Spenser's fellow student at Cambridge, Edward Kirke. Some, however, attribute the identity of E.K. to Spenser himself. Along with interpreting the eclogues, the glosses also give the identity of a number of characters such as Colin Clout (being Spenser), Hobbinol (being Spenser's friend Gabriel Harvey), etc.

What chiefly concerns us, though, is the identity of Pan. Although Pan has a number of identities **in this allegory** such as a Greek god and Henry VIII, **the most frequently used representation is that of Christ.** This allegory, in fact, has much to say about Christian virtues such as grace and kindness, as exemplified by Jesus Christ. Although the decision of Robert Barker to use this so-called Pan Headpiece (borrowed from Richard Field – see Appendix A) is open to question due to it's connotations with Greek mythology, it appears that it's inclusion in the 1611 expanded edition of Edmund Spenser's The Faerie Queene provided the impetus for Barker to do likewise.

Excerpts from the Gloss: The Shepheardes Calender: May

Great pan is Christ, the very God of all the shepheards, which calleth himselfe the greate and good shepherd. The name is most rightly (me thinkes) applied to him, for **Pan signifieth all or omnipotent, which is onely the Lord Jesus**...By which Pan, though of some be vnderstoode the great Satanas, whose kingdome at that time was by Christ conquered, the gates of hell broken vp, and death by death deliuered to eternall death, (for at that time, as he sayeth, all Oracles surceased, and enchaunted spirits, that were wont to delude the people, thenceforth held theyr peace) & also at the demaund of the Emperoure Tiberius, who that Pan should be, answere was made him by the wisest and best learned, that it was the son of Mercurie and Penelope, **yet I think it more properly meant of the death of Christ, the onely and very Pan, then suffereing for his flock.**

Part 8 – A Response to David Bay's claim

Excerpts from the Argvment: The Shepheardes Calender: December

The gentle shepheard satte beside a springe,
All in the shadowe of a bushy brere,
That *Colin* hight, which wel could pype and singe,
For he of *Tityrus* his songs did lere.   Tityrus = Chaucer

O soueraigne *Pan* thou God of shepheards all,
Which of our tender Lambkins takest keepe:
And when our flocks into mischaunce mought fall,
Doest save from mischiefe the vnwary sheepe:

I wont to raunge amydde the mazie thickette,
And gather nuttes to make me Christmas game:
And ioyed oft to chace the trembling Pricket,
Or hunt the hartlesse hare, til shee were tame.

The grieslie Todestool growne there mought I se
And loathed Paddocks lording on the same.
And where the **chaunting birds** luld me a sleepe,
The **ghastlie Owle** her grieuous ynne doth keepe.

My **boughs with bloosmes** that crowned were at firste,
And promised of **timely fruite** such store,
Are left both bare and barrein now at erst:
The flattring fruite is fallen to grownd before.   (Emphasis mine)

Note the **common elements** of the Pan Headpiece and this Argument. Keep in mind that we are dealing with the interpretation of symbols. Spenser uses Pan to represent Jesus Christ. Is David Bay not on dangerous ground in seeing giant phalli on the Pan figure when apparently no one else does, unless prompted by Bay's visualization techniques (see part 12).

Part 9 – A Response to David Bay's claim

that "the Baphomet-Goatshead-Devil's Head Banner is in the 1611 and 1619 KJV Bibles (because) Sir Francis Bacon, King James I, and the Knights of the Helmet (planned) to produce a Rosicrucian Mystic Bible. From Article 1004, page 1-4.

We now come to David Bay's latest Rosicrucian shibboleth – the goat's head of Baphomet, created in the fertile imagination of one Alphonse Louis Constant (1810 -1875, a.k.a. Eliphas Levi, the Hebrew transliteration of Constant's first two names), a French magician who created this winged androgynous humanoid goat c/w various accoutrements – which David assures us with great enthusiasm is depicted (c/w giant, though unseen, phallus of course) in the 1611 and 1619 KJV Bible.

Again, the fact that no one else sees this benign, innocuous banner of a goat's head in these KJV woodcuts as a malevolent Devil's device doesn't deter David.

Benign
Goat's Head Banner (1611 KJV) >>
printed by: Robert Barker

Malevolent
Goat's Head Banner (L'Artenice) >>
printed by Edward Allde

Part 9 – A Response to David Bay's claim

Here are the problems with David's reasoning:

1. Any human features in the KJV goat's head banner arguably resemble King James I more than Alphonse's dubious gift to the art world. As a matter of fact, books on physiognomy were popular in Europe at that time,,,some such as Porta's *Della Fisionomia Dell'Huomo* (1610) depicted anatomical comparisons between personages and animals.

2. David, the consummate flummoxer, opines (using the "power" of suggestion) that there are "striking similarities between the known Satanic symbol of Baphomet, at the left, and the KJV Goatshead on the right. Note the similarities:"

David's "Similarities"	My Comments
The eyes are set the same way on the head.	Yes, they are side by side. So what? Unless we are talking about a one-eyed Cyclops that's what we expect to see.
The nose is shaped the same.	Actually, no they aren't. The nose on Baphomet is noticeably wider. This is very evident if one looks at the statue on www.satanic-kindred.org/baphomet.htm
The jaw is shaped the same.	Again, I disagree. Like the nose, the jaw is noticeably wider on Baphomet.
Both goatsheads have a striking goatee protruding out from the chin.	So does our pastor, but since he stands six-foot-three-inches and weighs about two hundred and seventy-five pounds, I am reluctant to draw that comparison.

In the interests of not being too confining in our comparisons, perhaps David Bay with a goatee would resemble Baphomet even more closely than my pastor. Hairy lower body? Dual nature...Mr. Bay/Ms. Creant?

3. David poses the question "What is a Devil's Goatshead symbol doing on the 'Easter Forever' page in the original 1611 Bible (page xxx)?" We have already shown, in a visual way, that this banner does not depict a "Devil's Goatshead symbol". In fact, **this emblem** (not symbol) **beautifully depicts the Day of Atonement**, thus its location following the passage on Easter! I'll explain.

In scripture, the goat is mentioned in a variety of ways, such as:
   i.   the he goat, or leader of the flock (Ezek. 34:17)
   ii.   the goat of the sin offering (Lev. 9:3)
   iii.   the rough goat (Dan. 8:21)
   iv.   the scapegoat (Lev. 16: 8, 10, 26)

Rather than looking for answers in all the wrong places (David's *modus operandi*), let's again look to the scriptures to explain the components of this emblem.

The best way to find the meaning of a word in the King James Version is by utilizing the rule of first reference. If we turn to the passage in Leviticus 9 noted above, and the more detailed passage in Leviticus 16, we are reminded about the specific way in which the Israelites had to conduct themselves on the Day of Atonement. Here are some points relative to this matter:

   i.   The high priest, having bathed, dressed in white linen garments (see KJV title page), symbolizing the holiness required for admission into God's presence (Hebrews 12:14).
   ii.   The high priest brought a bullock for a sin offering, at his own cost, to offer for himself and his family; two goats for a sin offering, and a ram for a burnt offering, at the public cost, to offer for the people.
   iii.   The high priest then presented the two goats before the Lord at the tabernacle door, and cast lots upon them, implying that Christ's sacrifice was "by the determinate counsel and foreknowledge of God" (Acts 2:23; 4:28). On one goat was written "for Jehovah" and on the other "scapegoat" (for complete sending away).
   iv.   After slaying the bullock and carrying out various prescribed activities inside and outside the holy of holies and around the mercy seat, the high priest killed the goat "for Jehovah" and sprinkled its blood with his finger on the front of the mercy seat, then seven times before the mercy seat upon the ground in front of it, eastward toward the veil. The remainder of the blood from the bullock and goat was then sprinkled on the holy place and the golden altar, and poured around the altar of burnt offering…the places defiled by the priest's and the nation's sins thus being made ceremonially fit for the indwelling of God.
   v.   The high priest then laid his hands upon the head of the scapegoat confessing over it all the sins of the people. It was then led out into the wilderness and let loose.

The slain goat typifies Jesus Christ's vicarious death on the cross and our union as believers with him (Romans 6:5-11); the scapegoat typifies his removal of our sin out of sight where no witness will rise in judgment against us (Psalm 103:12). The head at the centre of this goat's head banner therefore represents Jesus Christ, the goat of the sin offering. The mis-shapen heads on either side of the centrepiece could therefore represent the scapegoat.

Psalm 103:12 tells us in this regard: "As far as the east is from the west, so far hath he removed our transgressions from us". Are not these grotesque heads on the "east" and "west" sides of the "wilderness" of this emblem?

In closing off this section of his Article 1004, David seems to have risen from the proverbial ashes, like the Phoenix Bird he claims to see on this emblem (this is a flower, David, not a bird). Discarding his failed pseudo-Icarus persona, our intrepid traveller has now found a new Greek god to impersonate...that being Morpheus, the god of dreams and moulder in allusion to the forms seen in those dreams.

After summarily declaring this emblem of Jesus Christ and the Day of Atonement as "utter blasphemy", pseudo-Morpheus is ready to spin his next dream for those not "blessed" with his "Left-Hand Vision".

We are now told, from Bay's vantage point on the left-hand path, that this emblem is filled with a plethora of "6's". The centre piece's horns form "6's", the vines form "6's", the "dragons" form "6's"...sixes here, sixes there, sixes and double sixes everywhere! Just like phalli, now David sees sixes everywhere. One hates to get too cynical, but what about all the other coils in this emblem that through this "lens" could be seen as "6's"? Does an open coil constitute a "6"? Does a mirrored image of an open coil constitute a "6"? Using pseudo-Morpheus' logic, there are literally millions of headpieces, tailpieces, ornamental borders and woodcut letters in books written over the last five hundred and fifty years that have "Satanic numerology" and through which "Bacon is symbolically repeating this goal (that Satan is going to establish his Perfect Government '66') three times, the maximum number of intensification allowed in occult art".

Not content with these rantings and ravings, David now sees "the two curling dragons (as) the occult symbol known as Ouroborus – the curling reptilian type creature." For one who claims to be such an adept at numerology, David seems to have forgotten that a "6" and a "0" are not the same thing (although David's "left-hand path" shows this to be a "9"). But why stop at "0", "6" and "9"? When I put on my Rose-Coloured glasses, I can see the rest of the numbers...and all the letters of the alphabet too!

By the way, this goat's head banner can be seen as a headpiece on *The Arraignment of Lewde, Idle, Froward, and Unconstant Women* by Joseph Swetnam, first published in London in 1615. The Dictionary of National Biography describes Swetnam's tome as a "coarse and violent attack on the fair sex" by a "woman-hater" who was one of the best known polemicists of the day.

Part 9 – A Response to David Bay's claim

There we go…another book by Francis Bacon and his Knights of the Helmet that, to quote David Bay, is "reverberat(ing) with occult power every second". Who knew?

Part 10 – A Response to David Bay's two claims about woodcut letters in the 1611 KJV:

From Article 1004, page 5-6: "The figure of Neptune (representing Satan) astride his horse and lifting his trident high is the woodcut for the first letter 'T' appearing on the title page of the Gospel of Matthew."

From Article 1004, page 6, there is a "demonic bat-like creature in the middle of the letter 'G' in the woodcut at the beginning of the Book to the Hebrews".

It is certainly appropriate that this part of the rebuttal is against David Bay in the guise of pseudo-Morpheus, as his first claim involves the Greek god Poseidon and Roman god Neptune. As is typical for those with ulterior motives, David Bay's claims are almost totally lacking in background. Background, if one considers the analogy of a painting, is critical in order to establish context. Without context, it is virtually impossible to ascertain meaning. This is the parallel world of Morpheus, the Rosicrucians, the Freemasons, the occultists and David Bay.

Let's stay in the real world, shall we? Here is some background information on early printing from *An Introduction to a History of Woodcut* by Arthur M. Hind, vol. 2, 1935, London.

Prints may be classed as (1) *relief-prints*, (2) *intaglio-prints*, (3) *surface-prints*, according to whether the black line of the design (ie. the part inked for printing) on the original block, plate or stone is (i) in relief, (ii) in intaglio (ie. cut into the surface), (iii) on the surface (ie. on a level with the rest of the surface). These divisions correspond roughly to (1) woodcut and wood-engraving, (2) engraving and etching on metal, (3) lithography.*

A metal plate cut, engraved or etched in relief is reasonably classed with woodcut and wood-engraving, just as lithography is generally held to include surface-prints from metal plates.*

In printing plates engraved or etched in intaglio, the ink is transferred to the paper not from the surface but from the furrows…and a special double-roller press is required of sufficient power to force the dampened paper into the furrows so as to pull out the ink…the ink will stand in relief of the paper.*

The printing of a woodcut is similar in method to printing from type, the ink being transferred from the surface of the parts in relief. The pressure applied is vertical…and the power required is considerably less than the double-roller copper-plate press. The ink is thicker and more sticky (sic) than that used in intaglio printing so that it may lie on the surface without flowing into the hollows.*
* Excerpts from page 1 and 2.

Part 10 – A Response to David Bay's two claims

With this information in mind, let's add some facts with respect to woodcut letters, the subject of this part of the rebuttal.

1. Ornamental woodcut initials required an artist and a cutter, craftsmen who were either employed directly or hired on piece-work contract by the printer. Artists did not necessarily work at the printer's establishment, but the cutters usually did. Many leading artists of the day, such as Albrecht Durer and Hans Holbein the Younger, worked as woodcut artists, and specialized in Biblical scenes.

2. The cutter used either a knife or a graver to accomplish his task. The knife was a flat piece of steel with its cutting edge at an acute angle to its back, and set in a wood handle. The graver was a small steel rod, of square or lozenge section, with its point sharpened in an oblique angle, with a flattened knob-shaped wood handle. A number of variations existed for the graver, depending on the detail of the cutting required as well as the species of wood and type of grain (flat or edge grain).

Fig. 4. Jost Amman. The Woodcutter.

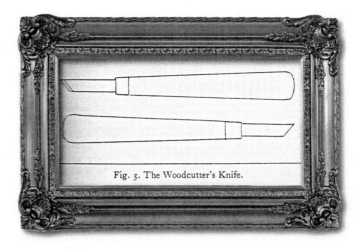

Fig. 5. The Woodcutter's Knife.

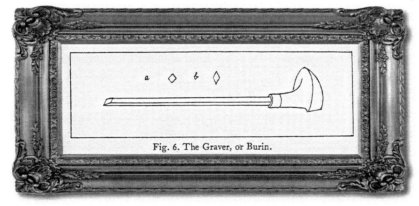

Fig. 6. The Graver, or Burin.

3. Printing houses were located in major cities throughout Europe, and some printers became extremely wealthy as the quality of their work increased in keeping with the skills of those who worked there. Printers such as Robert Estienne (Stephanus) were accomplished linguists and scholars, and became famous for their production of Greek and Latin New Testaments, Polyglot Bibles and the like.

4. Other printers, such as Christopher Plantin, specialized in the production of woodcut initials, which were used in books published in Venice, Paris, Lyons, Antwerp, Frankfurt, Amsterdam, London and elsewhere. These woodcut initials, or letters, were made in groups, or series, consisting of varying sizes, styles, decorative themes and borders. A book entitled *Ornamental Initials: The Woodcut Initials of Christopher Plantin* by Stephen Harvard gives examples of fifty-eight different series of these woodcut letters – some series having all of the letters of the alphabet and some only one. Of special interest with regard to our topic are the various themes depicted in each series – from floral to animal, from historical to mythical, from Biblical to what one could call medieval/grotesque.

5. As a rule, the printers seemed to make an attempt to fit the theme, or artwork, of these decorative woodcut initials to the subject matter of the book. When it came to large folio editions of major works (major works usually contained an elaborate copperplate or woodcut title page), however, this was not always possible...especially if this major work was a first folio edition of a Bible version requiring woodcut letters at the beginning of books and book chapters.

6. After carefully examining all of the woodcut letters throughout a facsimile of the 1611 First Folio Edition of the King James Version, it is obvious that Robert Barker, the printer of the KJV (along with any printers he used to assist him in the work), did not have enough woodcut letters of one series to complete his task. He therefore had to use a variety of letters from his inventory in order to get this First Folio Edition, first printing, off the presses without delay due to the pressure being exerted by King James to do so.

A number of woodcut letters were used throughout the text of the 1611 KJV which obviously differ significantly from the appearance of the majority. These differences are evident with respect to the borders, the letter style and the theme, or depiction, of the decorative imagery.

Before we examine these out-of-place letters, let's increase our understanding of the printing process in 1611. In order to do this, it is important to realize that the printer not only involves more than one person, but more than one function. There are, in fact, three key functions of the printing process – the compositor, the proof-reader and the distributor of the type. David Norton, in *A Textual History of the King James Bible*, informs us with regard to the critical nature of the first two:

> Compositors take type, a character at a time, from a case, a two-part box with compartments for each character. Printers did not have enough type to set the whole of the Bible at once, so parts had to be set and printed, then the type distributed to the case so that fresh text can be set. The apprentice distributing the type might mis-identify a character and so place it in the wrong compartment, or he might simply misplace a character. Consequently a compositor could reach into the correct compartment and pull out an incorrect character...

> After the compositor, the proof-reader has prime responsibility for seeing that the text is as it should be. We can never tell how *badly* the compositor worked because the proof-reader removed an unknown number of his mistakes. For the same reason, we can never tell how *well* the proof-reader worked: we cannot see what he did, only what he failed to do.

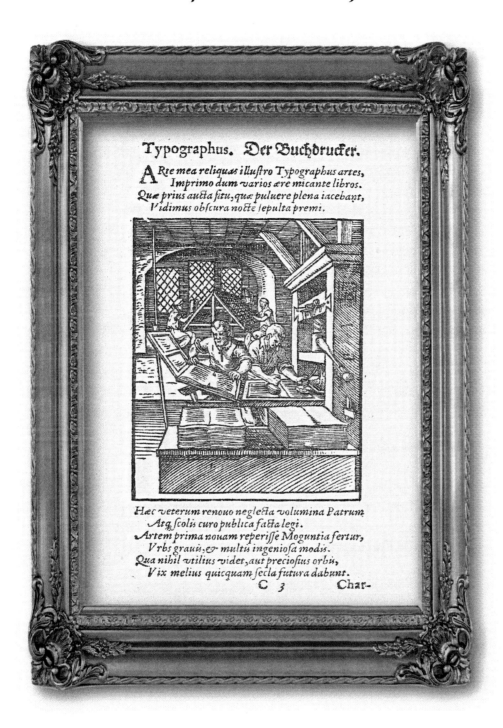

Typographus. Der Buchdrucker.

ARte mea reliquas illustro Typographus artes,
Imprimo dum varios ære micante libros.
Quæ prius aucta situ, quæ puluere plena iacebant,
Vidimus obscura nocte sepulta premi.

Hæc veterum renouo neglecta volumina Patrum,
Atg scolis curo publica facta legi.
Artem prima nouam reperisse Moguntia fertur,
Vrbs grauis, & multis ingeniosa modis.
Qua nihil vtilius videt, aut preciosius orbis,
Vix melius quicquam secla futura dabunt.
C 3   Char-

Hopefully the reader now has a somewhat better understanding than before of the difficulties with respect to securing the required number of large woodcut letters in a project such as this, and the potential for human error with regard to the selection and placement of text.

Part 10 – A Response to David Bay's two claims

Let's now examine the woodcut letters at the beginning of books and book chapters of the 1611 KJV that obviously don't belong with the majority – the majority being a variety of series of woodcut letters consisting of a similar floral motif. The first "hiccup", incidentally, with respect to the printer running out of like woodcut initials is at Chapter 4 of 2 Chronicles.

Although the floral motif on the letter "M" remains, the woodcut has a double-lined border. This lined border results in this woodcut taking up six lines of text, rather than the standard five lines for chapter beginnings. This "lined M" next occurs at 2 Chronicles Chapter 35. A double-lined "N" occurs at Nehemiah Chapter 10. A four-line "O" occurs at Esther Chapter 8.

These anomalies become more frequent as we get into Job, as the printer is obviously running out of many of the "proper" woodcut letters for chapter beginnings. As we come to the Psalms, we find a nine-line high woodcut initial at the beginning of chapter 1 that is unlike those at the beginning of the previous books of the Old Testament. As we page through the Psalms, we encounter numerous sizes and styles of woodcut initials – but all with the floral motif. That is, until we get to Psalm 141. Lo and behold, our "friend" Pan arrives on the scene!

This woodcut of Pan is not only higher (seven lines) but also wider than any chapter-beginning woodcut. Although the floral motif is again present, most initials, other than some small angelic-looking beings at the top of some initials, have been devoid of human or animal images until this one.

I suppose we have a choice to make here. Either:

1. Ali Baba and the forty thieves (sorry, that should be Francis Bacon and the Knights of the Helmet) broke into Robert Barker's print shop, stole twenty-one woodcut letters (see list of mismatched, inappropriate woodcut letters below) and substituted other letters, which escaped the notice of the compositor and proof-reader, or

2. The printer ran out of floral-motif letters as he came to the end of the first setting of print (that being half-way through the Bible at the end of the book of Proverbs) and especially so as he came to the end of the second setting of print (starting with Romans), and rather than making the effort to track down twenty-one more woodcut letters with floral motifs only, made the decision to go with what he had in his shop, or at least what was readily available.

Robert Barker was the King's Printer, with a prestigious commission with regard to the printing of something which obviously would create a large fanfare and resulting acclaim for him and his establishment. I believe that professional pride over-rode "humbling himself" and going to another printer for the twenty-one "proper" woodcut letters.

Part 10 – A Response to David Bay's two claims

Could the reason that Robert Barker chose to insert the Pan Headpiece at the end of the book of Acts have something to do with indicating where his soon-to-be-evident problems with the shortage of "Chapter 1" woodcut letters began? One could easily make the case that all of the images on the inappropriate letters are mythological in origin, just like the Pan Headpiece.

Let's first view a chart for the mismatched, but appropriate woodcut letters.

LETTER	LOCATION	DEPICTION
F	Luke Chapter 1 1 Thessalonians 2*	Luke, with his emblem, the ox
I	John 1	John, with his emblem, the eagle
I	Daniel 1 Zechariah 1 Judeth 1	Angelic heralds

* Although this image of Luke with his emblem, the ox, is obviously out of place with respect to the text, it is not inappropriate in the sense of those letters in the following chart.

Part 10 – A Response to David Bay's two claims

Let's now view a chart for mismatched and inappropriate woodcut letters.

LETTER	LOCATION	DEPICTION
A	Revelation 13	Winged humanoid
G	Hebrews 1	Winged humanoid
L	Wisdom of Solomon Psalm 141 1 Peter 3	Pan, from Greek mythology
O	Isaiah 64	King, possibly mythological
P	Romans 1	Daphne, from Greek mythology

LETTER	LOCATION	DEPICTION
P	1 Corinthians 1 Ephesians 1 1 Thessalonians 1 Titus 1	Athena, from Greek mythology
P	2 Corinthians 1 Galations 1 Philippians 1 Colossians 1 2 Thessalonians 1 Philemon 1 Peter 1	Cherubs with pitchforks... mythological?
S	2 Peter 1	Winged? humanoid
T	Matthew 1 Revelation 1	Neptune, or Poseidon, with sea horses from Roman/Greek mythology

Notice the following facts from the above charts:

1. The main problem with the shortage of woodcut letters involved those letters at "chapter one" locations – twenty-two to be exact. Out of a total of twenty-seven mismatched letters, this accounts for all but five.

2. The second obvious problem with the shortage of woodcut letters involved the letter "P" Twelve mismatched letter "P's" occur, out of a total of twenty-seven mismatched letters.

So there we have it...the story of the mismatched woodcut letters in the 1611 KJV...some appropriate, but the majority inappropriate for use in such an important publication, especially considering its significance to Bible-believing Christians for generations to come.

It's left up to the reader to decide...

Rosicrucian/Masonic/Kabbalistic/occultic plot by Francis Bacon or a poor decision by the printer?

Part II – A Response to David Bay's claim

that "the famous Rosicrucian-Baconian banner called 'Light A – Dark A'" (the signature of Francis Bacon and the Knights of the Helmet) appears "in the 1619 KJV, at the bottom of the Genealogies page". From Article 1004, page 7.

ebastian Brant, in 1494, published a book of one hundred and twelve chapters entitled *The Narrenschiff*, or Ship of Fools. Each chapter consists of a moral or Biblically-based proverb, followed by an illustration, then the chapter title and finally the poetical narrative.

According to Edwin Zeydel, the translator of *The Narrenschiff* into English, Brant's work is unique because of "its conception, without perspective, of the sins, faults, and foibles of its own day as exemplifications of folly – 'Narrheit'; its humble quotable sententiousness; its broad scope of types; its suggestive but never exhaustive treatment of subjects; its skilful versification; and the fact that it treats all estates alike, from the highest to the lowest, including even Brant himself, who delights…in referring to his own folly.

Another very important reason, no doubt, for the success of the work is the fact that it is a picture book, that each fool is depicted in an interesting woodcut, alone or in a group."

Part II – A Response to David Bay's claim

I'd like to dedicate the following excerpts from Chapter 102: **Of Falsity and Deception** from Sebastian Brant's work to those we have exposed who are engaged in this type of behaviour.

> Deceivers many, cheats I see,
> They join the dunce's revelry.
> False counsel, love, false friends, false gold,
> The world is full of lies untold.
> Fraternal love is dead and blind,
> Each one conspires to cheat his kind,
> That he may never lose, but gain,
> Though hundreds suffer ruin, pain.
>
> False money crops up unabated,
> False counsel, too; monk, priest, Beguine,*
> Lay brothers, they are false, unclean,
> For wolves in sheep's clothes now are seen.
>
> No trade is what it's claimed to be,
> Men sell their wares with falsity,
> Dispose of them with zealous skill
> Although their quality be nil.
>
> The Antichrist it doth forbode,
> His dealings take a devious road,
> His thoughts and acts and words forsooth
> Are turned to falsehood, base untruth.

* Sisters not bound by perpetual vows, but established for devotion and charity. They enjoyed a bad reputation as beggars, intriguers, and matchmakers. (From commentary – p. 388).

It is doubtful that these excerpts will have any mnemonic value for David Bay, but there's always hope. Anyway, we now (not surprisingly) find David bringing the "A-A" Printers' Device or "Light A – Dark A" Headpiece to our attention. As with the "Pan Headpiece" (as David has pointed out), Rosicrucians, Baconians and Freemasons (and obviously their fellow voyageur David) embrace this "A-A" Device as if it's the legendary Holy Grail in their attack on the King James Version.

As usual, David quotes a Rosicrucian/Baconian authority (Peter Dawkins) and a Masonic authority (Walter Mather) in his unrelenting, but futile, attempt to discredit the King James Version.

Part II – A Response to David Bay's claim

After reading through approximately ten websites and six books dealing with the Baconian bafflegab on this "A-A" Printers' Device, I'll put my response in point form as follows:

1. The majority of Baconians trace the origin of this device to one of the emblems created by Andreas Alciat (or Alciatus, Alciato, Alciati), which was then adapted by Geffrey Whitney, and incorporated into his emblem book titled *A Choice of Emblemes*, which was first published in Leiden in1586.

2. This "Light A – Dark A" shows up on two sides of a pyramid within an emblem about a "greedie sowe". Failing to accept the obvious, that Alciat's interest in Egyptian hieroglyphics led him to put his initials on the pyramid and that a sow does not necessarily "produce" Bacon; Smedley, Pott, Dawkins, Clifton, Walker, Ledsem, Weir, and of course Bay, fire up the barbecue nonetheless.

3. This "Light A – Dark A" was developed into a formal woodcut headpiece by one of the London printers, seemingly John Wolfe, and was soon copied by others, and shows up in dozens, if not hundreds, of books from the 1580's through to the mid-1600's.

4. Rosicrucians and Freemasons refer to the comments of Camden, in his work *Remaines Concerning Britaine*, published in 1614, as to one interpretation of the formalized "Light A – Dark A" Headpiece. In commenting on the subject of emblems, Camden gave the following as an example: "Variete and vicissitude of humane things he seemed to shew which parted his shield, Per Pale, Argent & Sables and counter-changeably writte in the Argent, Ater and in the Sables **Albus**". Thus, Camden is saying that **the "Light A" is A**ter **and the "Dark A" is A**lbus. Predictably, Smedley is quick to say that this "does not afford any satisfactory explanation as to why they are so used".

Part II – A Response to David Bay's claim

5. How do Rosicrucians, Baconians and Freemasons (and those who parrot them) expect to be taken seriously by anyone else when their leaders make statements such as the following:

Example No. 1:

In all probability, the keys to the Baconian riddle will be found in classical mythology. He who understands the secret of the Seven-Rayed God will comprehend the method employed by Bacon to accomplish his monumental labour.

> From *The Secret Teachings of All Ages* by Manley P. Hall. Bacon, Shakespere, and the Rosicrucians, page 168.

Example No. 2:

Peer deeply into certain parts of the dark pool of Elizabethan society, and like a fish swimming up from the depths, the form of this secret group begins to take shape. But then, of course, you have to know where to look.

> From *Francis Bacon & the Secret of Ornamental Devices* by Mather Walker. Part 1, page 20.

Example No. 3:

It will eventually be proved that the whole scheme of the Authorized Version of the Bible was Francis Bacon's.

> From *The Mystery of Francis Bacon* by William T. Smedley.

Part II – A Response to David Bay's claim

On a personal note, I recently purchased and sent down to Dr. D. A. Waite of the Dean Burgon Society and Bible For Today, an original booklet, printed in 1613, of *A Sermon Preached in Saint Maries Church in Oxford*, March 26, 1612, at the funeral of **Thomas Holland**, Doctor of the Chaire in Divinitie, and Rector of Exeter College, by **Richard Kilbie**, Doctor of Divinity, Rector of Lincolne College.

These two distinguished scholars and theologians served together on the Oxford Old Testament Committee of translators for the King James Version. The text for Dr. Kilbie's sermon was 1 Corinthians 15: 55, 56, 57:

> *O death where is thy sting? O grave, where is thy victory?*
> *The sting of death is sinne; and the strength of sinne is the law.*
> *But thanks be unto God, which hath given us victory through our Lord Jesus Christ.*

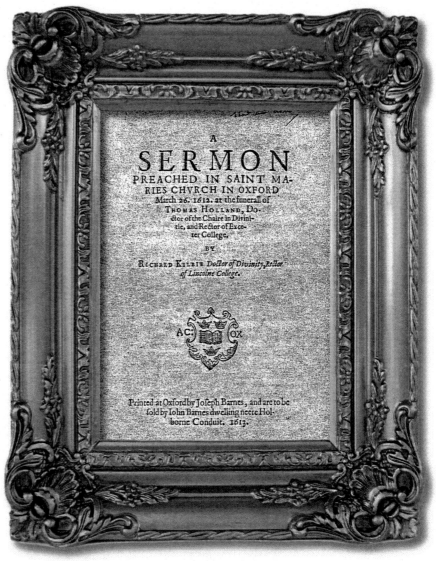

Above these words is the "Light A – Dark A" Headpiece. Does any thinking person (other than David Bay and his "friends") really believe that Francis Bacon and his Knights of the Helmet put their "signature" on the printing of this funeral sermon?

Perhaps some things in Elizabethan society, especially when they involve speculation, deception, conjecture and the like, are best left in the "dark pool" where they belong!

Part 12 – A Response to David Bay's claim

n part 11 of this rebuttal we found that David Bay, our intrepid traveller, was "at sea" with a large company of like-minded passengers. It seems that he is now back on dry land with an inclination to put his four years of army intelligence experience in cryptography to work.

Who would have believed (other than Bay and his Rosicrucian-Masonic-Baconian allies) that we needed to declare war on the King James Version of the Bible? A top-secret meeting of the minds in "naval intelligence" has apparently given David his marching orders, and who better to again join hands in "unholy matrimony" with but his Masonic cheerleaders from the deck of *The Narrenschiff*?

Perhaps David Bay sees himself as a modern-day Francis Bacon, who has received "the lamp of tradition". Consider the following excerpt from

www.sirbacon.org/links/dblohseven.html.

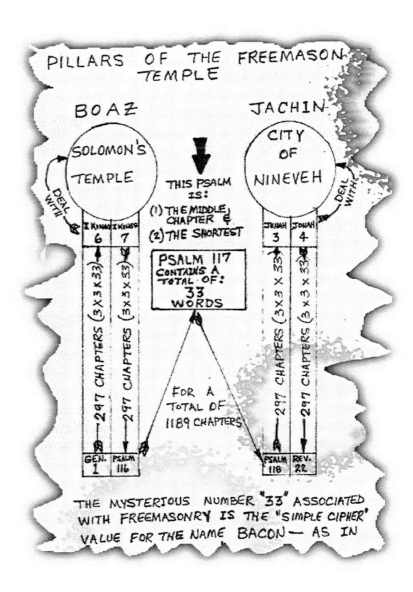

Illustration from Cutting Edge Article 1005:
DAVID BAY'S BLASPHEMOUS VISUALIZATION!

On page seven of this article on Francis Bacon and John Dee, we read:

> Manley P. Hall had a book, *Orders of the Universal Reformation*, in which a woodcut
> from 1655 by Jacob Cats shows an emblem of an ancient man bearing a likeness to
> John Dee, passing the lamp of tradition over an open grave to a young man with an
> extravagantly large rose on his shoe buckle In Bacon's sixth book of the *Advancement of
> Learning* he defines his method as *Traditionem Lampadis*, the delivery of the lamp.

> Mrs. Henry Pott writes in *Francis Bacon and His Secret Society*, "The organization or
> method of transmission he (Bacon) established was such as to ensure that never again
> so long as the world endured, should the lamp of tradition, the light of truth, be darkened
> or extinguished."

Part 12 – A Response to David Bay's claim

Take a look through the Bibliography for this article at the bottom of page seven. Perhaps David, in quoting from the Rosicrucian/Masonic/Baconian authors listed therein, feels that he is the One (remember the *Matrix* trilogy?) to save us from ourselves, and the parallel world we (meaning David) find ourselves in.

There is a Moody Blues album cover which has a similar rendition of the Jacob Cats woodcut. It's entitled *Every Good Boy Deserves Favour*. Perhaps David sees himself as the young boy receiving the lamp of tradition, and the hidden wisdom contained within, from an aged Francis Bacon, one who has been given an extreme makeover, of course, by the cheerleaders on board *The Ship of Fools*.

Part 12 – A Response to David Bay's claim

It's probably just me, but when I hear the word "cipher", my thoughts go back to a series of episodes from *The Beverly Hillbillies*, where Jethro is into ciphering and being a "double-nought spy".

Granny: They call them hills? Why, we've got moles that can push up higher ridges than that.

David's extreme makeover, it seems, also involves a change of colour to "Satanic Red". According to page 2 of his Article 1005, the "inspiration" for the title of this article, that being **"Don't Read Your Bible - - Count It"**, came from none other than **"an occultist with the handle of 'Satanic Red'"**. At least at this point, in David's last article, he is finally coming right out with his source of "wisdom" – the lamp of tradition which he is using involves hidden wisdom from Satanic sources. He is now so emboldened (and engorged with visions of giant phalli) that **he now sees the entire text of the 1611 King James Version as being represented by two giant phallic symbols with the Masonic Generative-principle symbol in between.**

In 2 Thessalonians Chapter 2, the apostle Paul, under the inspiration of the Holy Spirit, has some pertinent things to say to us regarding "the mystery of iniquity" as exemplified in Bay's latest delusion.

> **vs. 9** Even him, whose coming is **after the working of Satan**, with all power and signs and lying wonders,

> **vs.10** And with **all deceivableness** of unrighteousness in them that perish; because they received not the love of the truth, that they might be saved.

> **vs.11** And for this cause God shall send them **strong delusion**, that they should **believe a lie**:

> **vs.12** **That they all might be damned who** believe not the truth, but **had pleasure in unrighteousness**. (emphasis mine)

If you think I'm exaggerating in drawing a comparison between vs. 12's "**pleasure in unrighteousness**" and **Bay's ebullient state of enthrallment** under the charms of occultist Elizabeth van Buren;

consider Bay's words:

Listen as van Buren gushes even more eloquently about the supreme importance of the number "33".

Since our semantically-challenged sage's latest chicanery rests on a word, or words, in Psalm 117 let's get down to business without further ado.

Bay's allegation (in again parroting his Rosicrucian, Masonic, Baconian, occultist and Satanist mentors, according to his own admission) is that the whole of scripture in the 1611 King James Version consists of two Masonic pillars (phalli) – one on the left consisting of Genesis 1 to Psalm 116 and one on the right consisting of Psalm 118 to Revelation 22 – with the Masonic Generative-principle symbol (testicle) in the middle represented by Psalm 117.

Bay then speculates and conjectures that "Psalm 117, being the 'odd' chapter of the 1189 (1188 plus 1), is positioned in the very middle…of the Bible…consisting of exactly 33 words", and "as we **visualize the two pillars framing the number 33**, we are viewing but one of the many elaborate 'look at me' signs intended by Bacon and his Knights of the Helmet who orchestrated them!" In other words, we need to engage in the practise of visualization in order to "see" the Bible for what it supposedly "really" is…Bay's alleged Rosicrucian masterpiece.

Preparing for Visualization:

Visualization is an important base skill to any magical system. Whether you prefer a system that is ritual based or psychically driven, you need a healthy amount of practice in creating with your mind. When you visualize during magic you are uniting the logical portion of your mind with the task of creating realistic images, and maintaining those images as if there were a realistic physical object. You are also entertaining the creative portion of your brain by including bright colors, original concepts, and on a whim conjurations.

The crux of Bay's blasphemous visualization is that "without the simple separation of the word 'forever' into 'for' and 'ever', Psalm 117 would not have been the perfect chapter to place in the middle, because it would have contained on 32 words, not 33".

<< 1611 KJV:
Psalm 117:1,2

Part 12 – A Response to David Bay's claim

In other words, Francis Bacon and his Knights of the Helmet not only substituted twenty-one large woodcut letters in the still of the night (see part 10 of rebuttal), they also separated the word "forever", which was the "normal English usage" into two words, "**for ever**", by repositioning four other letters of text. How likely is this scenario? Consider the following:

1. The four verses following Psalm 117:2, those being Psalm 118: 1, 2, 3, and 4 all have the phrase "his mercy endureth for ever". Notice that "**for ever**" is in two words in all four of these verses. More Masonic manipulation?

2. The shepherd's psalm, Psalm 23, closes with "and I will dwell in the house of the Lord **for ever**". More manipulation by Francis Bacon and the Knights of the Helmet?

3. The Lord's prayer, in Matthew 6:13, closes with "but deliver us from evil: For thine is the kingdom, and the power, and the glory, **for ever**. Amen." Another example of Rosicrucians at work?

4. The guarantee of the preservation of the scriptures in Psalm 119:89 reads: "**For ever**, O Lord, thy word is settled in heaven." Were occultists at work here too?

5. In Revelation 22:5, we find the true source of light, the true Light-giver (as opposed to Lucifer, the false light-bearer of the lamp of tradition). Here is what the apostle John declares, under the inspiration of the Holy Spirit: "And there shall be no night there; and they need no candle, neither light of the sun; for the Lord God giveth them light: and they shall reign **for ever and ever.**

This last passage of scripture gives a clue as to the structured meaning of the term "for ever". The Gage Canadian Dictionary, which reflects the English of Great Britain much more closely than American dictionaries, has "<u>for</u> always, **without** <u>ever</u> coming to an end" as the first meaning of "**forever**", the single-word structure that "is the **normal English usage**" of today.

For proof that he term "**for ever**", in two words, was "**normal English usage**" in 1611, I refer again to a copy I have, made **from the original 1613 printing** of "*A Sermon Preached in Saint Maries Chvrch in Oxford* March 12, 1612, at the funeral of Thomas Holland, Doctor of the Chaire of Divinitie, and the Rector of Exeter College, by Richard Kilbie, Doctor of Divinity, Rector of Lincolne College", with the "Light A – Dark A" Headpiece (supposedly a signature of Francis Bacon), I quote from page 13: "*O Death, where is thy sting?* Thou maiest indeed sting our bodies unto death; but thou haste lost thy great sting, thou canst not now **any more** sting our soules to death. O Tyrant, thou mayst kill our bodies for a time, but thou canst not kill our soules **for ever**."   (Note the separation in "**any more**" as well as in "**for ever**".)

Passage from >>
Dr. Kilbie's 1612 sermon

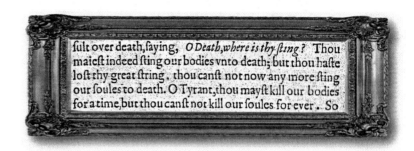

I close this rebuttal with both encouragement and a warning from **Psalm 37:7-18** in God's word, the 1611 King James Version. As the saying goes, "if the shoe fits, wear it".

7   Rest in the Lord, and wait patiently for him: fret not thyself because of him who prospereth in his way, because of the man **who bringeth devices to pass**.

8   Cease from anger, and forsake wrath: fret not thyself in any wise to do evil.

9   For evildoers shall be cut off: but those that wait upon the Lord, they shall inherit the earth.

10 For yet a little while, and the wicked shall not be: yea, thou shalt diligently consider his place, and it shall not be.

11 But the meek shall inherit the earth; and shall delight themselves in the abundance of peace.

12 **The wicked plotteth** against the just, and gnasheth upon him with his teeth.

13 **The Lord shall laugh** at him: for he seeth that his day is coming.

14 **The wicked have drawn out the sword**, and have bent their bow, to cast down the poor and needy, and to slay such as be of upright conversation.

15 **Their sword shall enter into their own heart**, and their bows shall be broken.

16 A little that a righteous man hath is better than the riches of many wicked.

17 For the arms of the wicked shall be broken: but the Lord upholdeth the righteous.

18 The Lord knoweth the days of the upright: and their inheritance shall be **for ever**.

The End

Appendix A

David Bay does a lot of huffing and puffing about the so-called Archer Device or Pan Headpiece, with the tag-line of "the hunt for Pan". As is typical in Rosicrucian and Masonic lore, however, we are never told the whole story - facts are always perverted, misinterpreted or altered in some way to fit the prescribed dogma - in this case Baconian mythology.

As it turns out, the Pan Headpiece is in fact two Pan Headpieces, an original one which is documented to be one of John Wolfe's ornamental devices, and an obvious copy which seemingly made its appearance in 1610.

One of the difficulties in determining the genealogy of the two Pan Headpieces is that the information is scattered throughout many reference books, and is incomplete at that.

The following chart represents the most complete record to date regarding this device - both the original and the copy - complete with the book title, date of publication and printer of the various books containing this device.

ORIGINAL PAN HEADPIECE			COPY OF PAN HEADPIECE		
Date of Publication	Book Title	Printer	Date of Publication	Book Title	Printer
C. 1580	Clinton, Purser and Arnold, To Their Countrymen, Their Unfeigned Penitence, etc.	John Wolfe			
1582	The Passionate Century of Love	John Wolfe			
1583	The Ancient Order, Societie and Unitie Laudable of Prince Arthure	John Wolfe			

Appendix A

ORIGINAL PAN HEADPIECE			COPY OF PAN HEADPIECE		
1588	Descrittione Del Regno Di Scotia (History and Chronicles of Scotland)	John Wolfe			
1595	The Lives of the Noble Grecians and Romanes	Richard Field	1610	The Catalogue of Honour	William Jaggard
1598	Aristotle's Politiques, or Discourses of Government, Translated out of Greeke into French.	Adam Islip	1614	History of the World by Sir Walter Ralegh	William Stansby
1601	The Parallel Rheims/Bishops Version English New Testament	George Bishop	1620	Novum Organum by Sir Francis Bacon	John Bill
1611	The Faerie Queene and the Shepheardes Calender, New Combined Edition, by Edmund Spenser	Humphrey Lownes	1623	Great Shakespeare Folio	Isaac Jaggard & Ed. Blount
1611	The Holy Bible, Conteyning the Old Testament, and the New (King James Version)	Robert Barker	1623	The Theatre of Honour and Knighthood	William Jaggard
1640	The History of the Jews	John Legate			

Appendix A

As mentioned in part 3 of this rebuttal, the more elaborate woodcuts were shared by many publishers and printers, and frequently spanned decades of use. In addition, printers served apprenticeships of up to seven years with various established printing houses before being entered in Stationers' Hall as a journeyman. Some became partners in the firm they apprenticed with, while others created new partnerships or bought the woodcuts and other devices from the estate of deceased printers.

In order to show the inter-relationships among the various printers involved with the 1611 KJV Pan Headpiece, I have created the following diagram. The dates indicate the period that the printer was actively engaged in printing books in England.

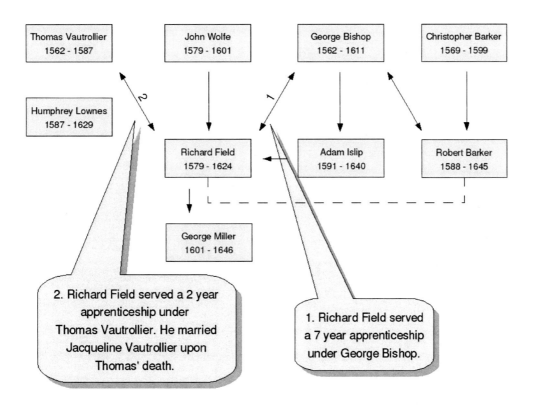

2. Richard Field served a 2 year apprenticeship under Thomas Vautrollier. He married Jacqueline Vautrollier upon Thomas' death.

1. Richard Field served a 7 year apprenticeship under George Bishop.

The purpose of this appendix is to show that ornamental devices such as the Pan Headpiece were tools of the London printing houses and not sigils, or seals, of Rosicrucian arcana or the "signature" of Sir Francis Bacon.

Appendix B

xamples of the "A-A" Headpiece used in books printed in England and having no proven association with Francis Bacon are as follows:

1. *L'Artenice* by Seigneur de Racan Bueil. Printed by Edward Allde, circa January 1626.
2. *La Muse Chrestienne* by Adrien de Rocquigny. Printed by George Miller in 1627.
3. *Rime* by Petruccio Ubaldini. Printed by Richard Field in 1596.
4. *A comparison of the English and Spanish nation: composed by a French Gentleman against those of the League*, Tr, by R. Ashley. Printed by John Wolfe in 1589.

Books printed by John Wolfe account for at least 9 books containing the A-A Headpiece.

5. *Of the diverse degrees of the ministers of the Gospell.* Tr. From Latin. Printed by John Wolfe, for George Bishop in 1590.
6. *Orlando Furioso* by Robert Greene. Printed by Richard Field in 1591.

Books printed by Richard Field account for at least seventeen of the books containing the A-A Headpiece. Field had at least three different A-A devices in his possession.

The A-A Headpiece is no different from a host of ornamental devices which are catalogued in books such as *Printers' & Publishers' Devices in England & Scotland, 1485-1640,* by Ronald B. McKerrow. This woodcut is part of the printer's repertoire of woodcut headpieces, tailpieces, borders and letters used long before Francis Bacon was born and long after he died.

The A-A Headpiece, like the so-called Pan Headpiece, was copied by many printers. I have not taken the time to trace the origin of the A-A Headpiece as I have the so-called Pan Headpiece, but there is no credible evidence of a sinister nature in its use, and especially not as a Rosicrucian or Baconian seal.

Appendix C

 s with the original Pan Headpiece and other woodcuts, the so-called goatshead banner was copied a number of times and used by at least two other printers in a variety of publications. It is important, therefore, to look at the original woodcut to determine if it's use had any contextual bearing with respect to the subject matter of the books in which it was used.

We have already determined that there is strong evidence to show that this was the case for both the Pan Headpiece and the goatshead banner.

As has been shown in part 9, there is an obvious difference in the appearance of the "benign" goatshead banner in the 1611 KJV and the "malevolent" goathead banner in Bueil's *L'Artenice*.

With this evident disparity in mind even between two closely related woodcuts, Bay's attempt to equate the 1611 KJV goatshead with Eliphas Levi's androgynous Baphomet goat is truly unconscionable.

Book Order Information